DATING
GRAY

SITUATIONSHIPS REVEALED

the color journal

BY:

RIIAN ALLIA

Riian Allia
© Copyright 2018 Riian Allia Whitby
ISBN: 978-0-9600313-1-3

Published by Lovd2Life, LLC
P.O. Box 6782 Edmond, OK 73083

www.lovd2life.com

For bulk orders or other inquiries, email:
lovd2life@gmail.com

welcome

Welcome sisters! If you're reading this, it's not too late. So let me start by saying that I'm glad you're here. Not here, as in your situation, but here... Reading *Dating Gray* and taking a step in finding the solution to your problem. You even took it a step further by using your fabulous journal! You go, girl!

Now, if you're participating in the #NoMoreGrayChallenge, it's probably because somewhere along the line, you've found yourself in a bit of a situation or, well, a "situationship." I realize that there may also be other gray areas in your life that have contributed to your struggles with relationships. If so, I can totally relate!

Dating Gray was written out of an extremely vulnerable place in my life. Throughout my teen years and young adulthood, I found myself involved in countless relationships that left me feeling worthless and unloved. At one point, I even sank into a deep depression, unable to see the purpose in my life. As God has brought me out of that place, I've witnessed a lot of teens, young adults, and grown women, walk into the same dark room.

I've held my sisters' hands, wiped their tears, and gave them comforting words but in the end, they would go right back to the same guy who broke their hearts. Their countenance changed and I cringed at the thought of them losing themselves time and time again, like me. So I wrote this book for them and sis, I wrote it for you. You are worth far more than the uncertainty and heartbreak that comes along with living a gray life! I realize that this will challenge you. It challenged me. But the outcome of living your life in color will be so worth it.

My prayer is that this journal will deepen your relationship with Christ by showing you how much He loves you so that you'll be able to see your value and never settle for counterfeit love again. Now that we've discussed the background, let's get down to business...

If you already think that this journal is doing the most [being extra, making you do work] you are absolutely correct! By nature, I am extra. I tend to do the most. So why wouldn't I do the most when it comes to helping my sisters grow in their relationship with our Heavenly Father? This, right here, is the definition of extra, sis. Oh, yes! And guess what? I need you to be extra with me! I need you to really put effort into this journal. In order for God to truly work through us, we have to also put in the work. I know, I know. "Work" isn't cute. "Work" can get messy before it gets clean and sometimes we don't enjoy making time for it, but work is necessary. You have to do the work, sis. There's no way around that. But I've tried my best, in all of my extra-ness, to make it slightly enjoyable for you.

Why should you color? First, colors can symbolize many things, as you have seen on your **color code** page. I want you to physically see the areas that you need to work on and the beauty of your colorful life. More importantly, I want you to look back on this, years from now, pass it along to your daughter, niece, cousin, friend or mentee, then show them the beauty of your journey. Talk about it. This is how they will know that you are not perfect. Your vulnerability may break the cycles that we're often too embarrassed or too proud to talk about. Call your dysfunction out by its name. Bring it from the darkness into the beauty of God's marvelous light. Break the cycles. Have the discussions. Speak your truth and ask God for wisdom and guidance.

The enemy would love for you to suffer in silence. He desires for you to be trapped in the dark but oh, sister, he's met his match with you. God is calling you out, in the best way! He's exposing the hidden things in your heart. But don't let that scare you away. I had to go through the same thing when I wrote this for you. So let my story help you be brave. I know it's hard sometimes but your freedom is worth it all. YOU are worth it ALL. Hey, Jesus thought so. He gave His life for your freedom! You are already free in Him.

Sometimes your past (or even your present) will make you think otherwise. Sometimes we have to journey back to the moments when we forgot about our freedom, when we gave it away, or even when it was taken from us. So this journal is not ordinary. No, sis. It's so extra. It won't turn out perfect and organized. You may forget to color some pages but I want you to try to color them all—in your own way. You need to be extra. This is your freedom we're talking about! So hey, if you need to color outside the lines, if your pages have teardrop stains on them, if your marker bleeds through the page, that's okay.

Let go of the misconception that your healing will be perfect. True healing may not be appealing to you but it's the only way that you will uncover the true masterpiece, the true resilience, the true beauty—you. So put your past, doubts, fears, confusion, anger, broken heart, joy, peace, wins, and healing on these pages. But don't hide them away for yourself. **Pass them on so that the women around you know that they're not alone.** You're not alone either! I'm here to help you but I know someone who can do way more than I could cover on these pages. Let God lead you through this journey. He's the only one who can transform your life and once you allow Him to work, you'll never be the same!

color code: spiritual significance of color

color in the boxes as you learn what each color represents...

rose	Rose of Sharon, The Father's Heavenly care over the lilies of the field: His children
pink	Joy, right relationship, compassion, heart of flesh, passion for Jesus, The Bridegroom's heart
wine	New wine, the cup of the new covenant, blessings of God, the fellowship of Christ's suffering
red	Blood of Jesus, covenant of grace, cleansing, justification, atonement, sacrifice, redemption, life, love, sovergin power, Christ the sacrificial lamb, courage, war, persecution
orange	The glory of God, Holy Spirit baptism, fiery passion, flaming throne of God, The temple of God, fall harvest, fruitfulness, healing, praise
peach	First love, praise
yellow	Joy, spiritual enlightenment, Shekinah Glory
olive	God's annointing, consecration
green	Eternal life, new life, vigor, prosperity, grace, mercy, restoration, healing, growth, wholeness, God's Holy Seed, sowing, new beginning, spiritual privileges, spiritual life
emerald	Presence, The Throne of God
pastel green	Comfort
turquoise	Open heaven, River of God, sanctification, healing, life-giving flow of the Holy Spirit, The New Jerusalem
light blue	Spiritual or heavenly realm, Holy Spirit, reconciliation, grace, peace

sapphire	The river of the Spirit, washing
blue	Revealed God, divine revelation, truth, grace, divinity, The Priesthood, authority, Messiah, power of the Holy Spirit, heaven, overcomer
indigo	Richness, abundance, infilling of the Holy Spirit
purple	Royalty, kingship, majesty, mediator, supernatural, wealth, dominion, Sonship, inheritance, repentance, authority, intercession, refuge
lavender	Love, passion, repentance, sorrow
iridescent	Symbol of God's truth, purity, breath of heaven, Wind of the Holy Spirit, overcoming power, glory, fruit of the Holy Spirit, cleansing, blessings of God, sanctification, The Bride of Christ, precious stones, hidden treasures
white	The Bride, purity, innocence, surrender, holiness, robes of righteousness, light, joy, angels, saints, peace, triumph, victory, completion
gold	Eternal Father, The Godhead, glory, purification, majesty, righteousness, divine light, trial by fire, victory
copper	Consuming fire, heaven
bronze	Righteous judgment of God, repentace, mercy seat
brown	Humility, submission, repentance, Godly offspring, humanity, spiritual death
black	Humility, the mysteriousness of God, darkness, sin, sorrow, calamity, affliction, mourning
rainbow	God's covenant promises, favor, joy of the Lord, faithfulness, freedom

guidelines
keep coloring, sis

chapter intro

The **chapter intro** will help you gauge your thoughts about the corresponding chapter in the Dating Gray book. I provide a brief summary just in case you need a refresher on what the chapter was about. You may be tempted to skip the intro, but don't do it! It will help get your mind right for the reflection.

color playlist

The **color playlist** is a list of songs (various genres), sermons, lessons, and mini motivational videos that spoke to me while I was writing each chapter. But this isn't really about me, so I made a space for you to write some songs and videos that helped you get through these seasons in your life. *Major Key: Don't choose music and videos that will get you back in your feelings. We're moving forward!

REFLECTION

Let's be honest here. Aside from all of the fun coloring pages, the **reflection** prompts are probably the main reason that you purchased this journal. I'm totally fine with that. So I think it's important that you take the prompts seriously. Answer them honestly. Really reflect on the questions/scriptures. Don't cheat yourself, sis. You need this.

prayers

There may be a prayer prompt in the activity section but I also want you to get into the habit of not being afraid or feeling inconvenienced by praying multiple times a day. The **prayers** section can be used to continue a prayer from an activity or write a completely new prayer. You can even use it to write down any response that God gives you. Just make sure that you practice praying regularly.

ACTIVITY

Each chapter **activity** will help you further break down the topics that were discussed in both the book and reflection prompts. The Number One Rule: ALWAYS USE COLOR.

chapter feels

You may be a creative person who doesn't like writing on neatly printed lines (that's totally me) or you may be someone who likes things that are more structured. You may like both, depending on the day. No matter what style you have when it comes to journaling, I wanted to make sure that you had the freedom to choose. **Chapter feels** is your ultimate journaling section. You can write, draw, use stickers, paint, or anything else you can think of. Just write down how you feel.

IN MY FEELINGS
scripture guide

Okay sis, let's be real. There are times when we will be **in our feelings** but I encourage you not to base your decisions off of them. When we're mad, we want to fight. When we're sad, we want to lock ourselves in our rooms and play depressing music that will validate our sadness. When we're happy, we tend to be nice and when we lack joy (or are just hungry), we're rude (usually with an attitude). See where I'm going here? For too long, we've acted out how we felt and in some cases, there's nothing wrong with that. But are our actions (caused by this rollercoaster of emotions) pleasing to God? We've *all* struggled in this area but we shouldn't let our feelings control our lives. If we do, we will likely end up in unhealthy cycles and be blind to what God is trying to do *through* us. So here are some scriptures to help you when you find yourself "in your feelings." Write them on notecards or say them out loud when you catch yourself slipping into another "in your feelings challenge."

ANGER	ANXIETY//STRESS	BROKEN HEART	COMPARISON	DOUBT	FAITH
Ephesians 4:26-31	Joshua 1:9	II Corinthians 4:8-10	II Corinthians 10:12	James 1:5-8	Hebrews 11:1-6
James 1:19-20	Matthew 6:34	Joel 2:25	Galatians 6:4-6	John 20:24-29	Isaiah 43:10
James 4:1-2	I Peter 5:7	Matthew 11:28	James 3:16-18	Mark 9:24	John 3:16-18
Matthew 5:22-25	Philippians 4:16	Psalm 34:18	Matthew 7:1-5	Matthew 14:31-33	John 14:1
Proverbs 19:11	II Timothy 1:7	Romans 8:18	Proverbs 14:30	Psalm 42:11	Mark 11:24

FEAR	FORGIVENESS	GUARDING YOUR HEART	HEALING	IDENTITY	JOY
Deuteronomy 31:8	Acts 3:19	Ephesians 6:11-18	Isaiah 61:1-3	II Corinthians 5:20-21	James 1:2-4
Isaiah 43:1	Colossians 3:13	Matthew 6:21	Jeremiah 17:14	Ephesians 2:10	I Peter 1:8-9
John 14:27	I John 1:9	Philippians 4:7	Matthew 8:8	5:1-2	Philippians 4:4-7
I John 4:18	Luke 17:3-4	Proverbs 3:5	I Peter 2:24	John 8:31-36	Psalm 30:4-5
Psalm 18:2	Matthew 6:14-15	Proverbs 24:3	Psalm 51:10	I Peter 2:9-10	Romans 15:13
				Psalm 139:13-18	

KEEPING GOD FIRST	KINDNESS	LOSS	LOVE	PEACE	PRAYER
Colossians 3:12-17	Ephesians 2:4-7	II Corinthians 1:3-4	I Corinthians 13:1-8, 13	Colossians 3:15	Hebrews 4:15-16
Mark 12:29-31	Ephesians 4:31-32	II Corinthians 6:4-10	I John 4:7-12	John 14:27	I John 5:14-15
Matthew 6:33	Galatians 5:22-23	Isaiah 49:13	Matthew 5:44-47	John 16:33	Matthew 6:5-13
Matthew 10:38-39	II Peter 1:3-9	Matthew 5:4	Matthew 22:37-37	I Peter 3:8-12	Matthew 7:7-8
Proverbs 3:5-6, 9-10	Titus 3:4-7	Psalm 119:50	Romans 8:38-39	Psalm 119:165	I Thessalonians 5:16-21

PURITY	REST	SADNESS	SHAME	TEMPTATION	WAITING ON GOD
Matthew 5:8	Exodus 33:14	Galatians 6:9	Hebrews 4:14-16	I Corinthians 10:12-13	Habakkuk 2:3
Philippians 4:8	Isaiah 26:3	Hebrews 10:35-36	I John 1:9	Hebrews 2:18	Hebrews 10:23
Psalm 19:14	Matthew 11:28-30	Isaiah 61:1-3	Matthew 18:12-14	James 1:13-14	Psalm 33:20
Psalm 26:2	Psalm 4:8	I Peter 4:12-13	Romans 6:12-23	I Peter 5:8-9	Psalm 62:5
Romans 12:2	Psalm 91:1-16	Psalm 23:4	Romans 8:1-17	II Peter 2:9	Psalm 130:5

Introduction

Hey Queen! You made it through the introduction. Now that wasn't so bad, was it? During the chapter, we briefly went over two main points: spiritual fruit and the definition of situationships. Now that you were able to read over the workbook guidelines and dip your feet in the calm waters of coloring, let's get to work. See how nicely I prepped you? *Wink, wink* But really sis, I cannot stress enough how important checking your fruit is. Often, we place the blame on the guys we've been with but in reality, we are also apart of the problem. If we're picking the same men over and over again, or even simply attracting the same type of guy, then there is still work that we need to do. There are still some areas of our lives that we have to allow God to clean up and make new. But first, I want you to take some time and reflect. It's super important to be honest with yourself. I know it's hard sometimes but if we ever want to break our situationship cycle then we have to begin with the truth. So pull out your big girl brushes and let's start painting honesty. It doesn't have to be cute or fit inside the lines. This is your story. Color it how you want. Are you ready? Let's go!

good fruit, bad fruit

We all know some examples of "bad fruit." If not, Galatians 5:19-21 says,
"When you follow the desires of your sinful nature, the results are very clear: sexual immorality, impurity, lustful pleasures, idolatry, sorcery, hostility, quarreling, jealousy, outbursts of anger, selfish ambition, dissension, division, envy, drunkenness, wild parties, and other sins like these."

But there's hope for us! Galatians 5:22-23 tells us what good fruit is: love, joy, peace, patience, kindness, goodness, faithfulness, gentleness and self-control. However, we can't produce these good fruits on our own. The Bible let's us know that good fruit can only come from the Holy Spirit.

REFLECTION

What are some struggle areas in your life that you need to produce good fruit in?

Think about the areas that God is already cleaning up in your life. **Write them down (to the right, to the right).**

What pattern have you noticed in your relationships? How did the pattern begin?

In this book, I formed my own definition of "situationship" but now it's your turn (ayyyyeee). **Write down your interpretation of what it means to be in a situationship.**

Now, write down why you shouldn't settle in a situationship.

But hold up. Wait a minute. I want you to take some time to relax and reflect...

Have you been trapped in a gray cycle?

1. Between each arrow, write down where the cycle began. Go back to your childhood if necessary. This activity may be difficult, but remember to be honest with yourself.

2. After completing the cycle think about how you feel. Now color each arrow in **red.**

3. Jesus died for your cycle. Let Him be the one to stop it because only He can. If you could stop, you probably would've done it by now. So let Him into your heart and ask for His help. You are free in Him! Allow Him to free you, sis!

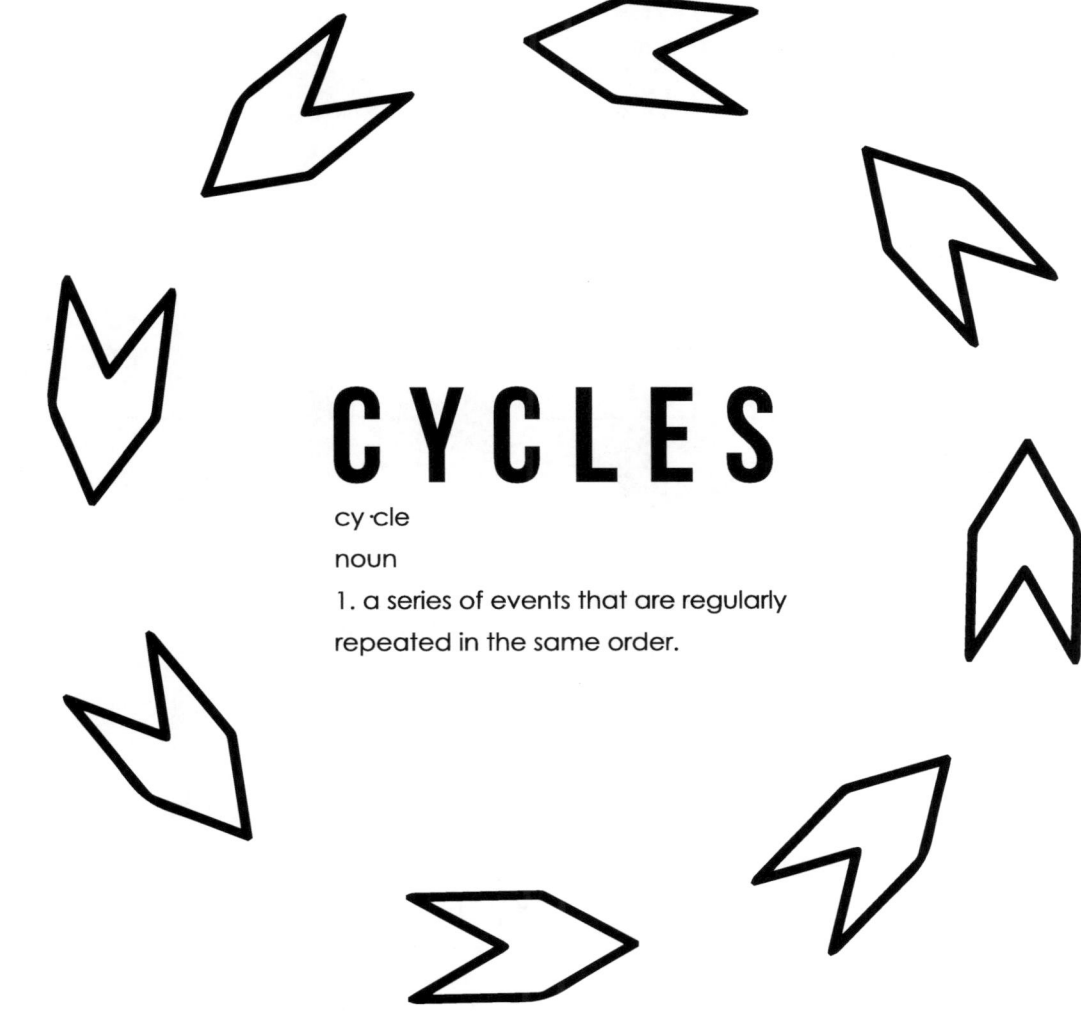

A
C
T
I
V
I
T
Y

CYCLES

cy·cle

noun

1. a series of events that are regularly repeated in the same order.

color playlist

COLOR PICK

JORDAN MAY // HEALING

DARIUS JAMES // KEEP ON RUNNING

JONATHAN MCREYNOLDS // CYCLES

TASHA COBBS-LEONARD // BREAK EVERY CHAIN

S
O
N
G
S

YOUR PICK

S
O
N
G
S

COLOR PICK

JOSEPH SOLOMON // HOW DO I GET RIGHT WITH GOD?

ALLYSON ROWE // IF YOU WANT A GODLY HUSBAND...

Y
O
U
T
U
B
E

YOUR PICK

Y
O
U
T
U
B
E

encouragement

Sis, I'm so excited for you! I've prayed for this moment—the moment that you finally began to realize your worth. There are so many things that God has in store for you. There's so much that He wants to reveal to you but you have to open your eyes.Ironically, you have to start by opening your eyes to you. I know, it sounds weird but you have to see who you are in this moment in light of who God has called you to be. There's a higher standard for you and Your Heavenly Father will show you how to get there. He'll teach you how to overcome. Just keep coloring!

prayers

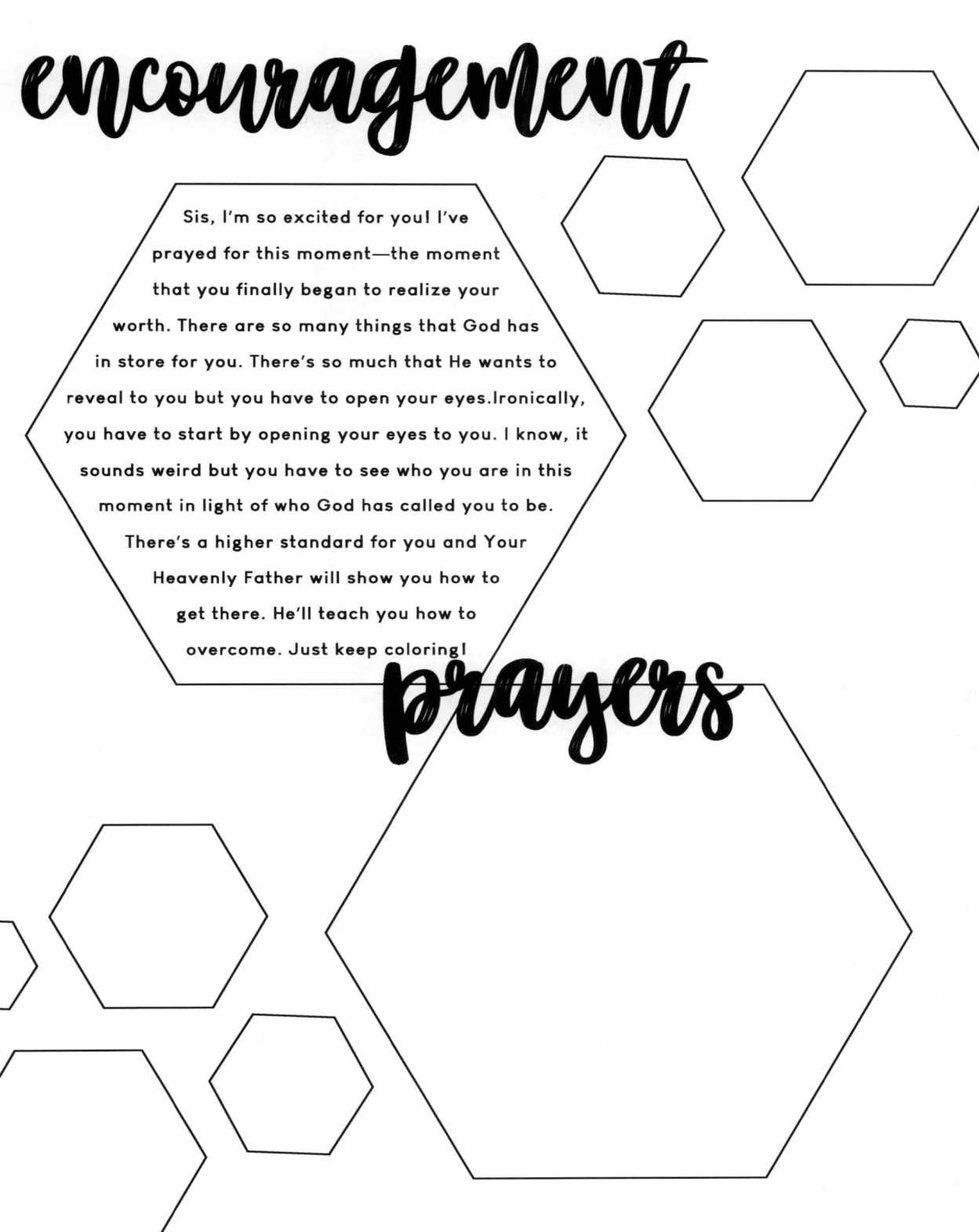

chapter *feels*

_____

_____

_____

_____

_____

_____

_____

_____

_____

_____

_____

defining gray

Okay sis, how do you feel? Good, indifferent? Right now I want you to do a heart check because that's exactly what I had to do. In this chapter, we defined "Gray" and discovered that it's the in-between. The uncertainty. The "I can get reeeeeally close to black some days and I can get reeeeeally close to white on other days" mentality. But can I tell you something? You deserve so much better than an unclear, unfulfilling relationship, even if it's the relationship you have with yourself. So why settle for gray. There's so much color waiting on the other side. So keep coloring, Queen. Keep on coloring.

love, love, love!

Okay, so in the last chapter, we talked about checking our fruit and the first fruit of the Spirit that's listed in the Bible is "love." In Mark 12:30-31, Jesus is commanding us to love God with all of our heart, soul, mind, and strength. Then He gives us a second commandment (which is equally important) "loving your neighbors as yourself."

Over the years, I realized that Jesus was intentional about the order of His commands. First, we are called to love God. When we experience the boundless love of Christ, we are able to learn from Him and see how much He loves us. As He teaches us to love ourselves, we are then equipped to love others, but not a moment before.

Often, we try to love others, ourselves, and then God last. Sis, this will never work. You have to start with God and keep Him first, always. His love **never** fails.

REFLECTION

List 5 ways that you can start/continue putting and keeping Our Daddy first in your life.

How did creating that list make you feel? What areas of your life have you put God on the backburner?

I Corinthians 13 paints a clear, colorful picture of Our Father's Love. **Take some time to write down what each description means to you. Circle the qualities that you would like to improve in green.**

Patient.

Kind.

Not envious.

Doesn't boast.

Isn't proud.

Isn't rude.

Isn't self-seeking (selfish)

Not easily angered.

Doesn't keep record of wrongs.

Doesn't delight in evil.

Rejoices with truth.

Always protects.

Always trusts.

Always hopes.

Always perseveres.

Never fails.

What areas of your life have you been living or dating Gray?

1. Write those areas next to each gray box (ex. I've been focused more on men than God).
2. Color the box beside it with a color from the color code list that represents how you want to cover the gray area (ex. Peach: Going back to my first love, Jesus).
3. Write action steps next to your colored box (ex. I ask for forgiveness, pray daily, and read the Bible daily).

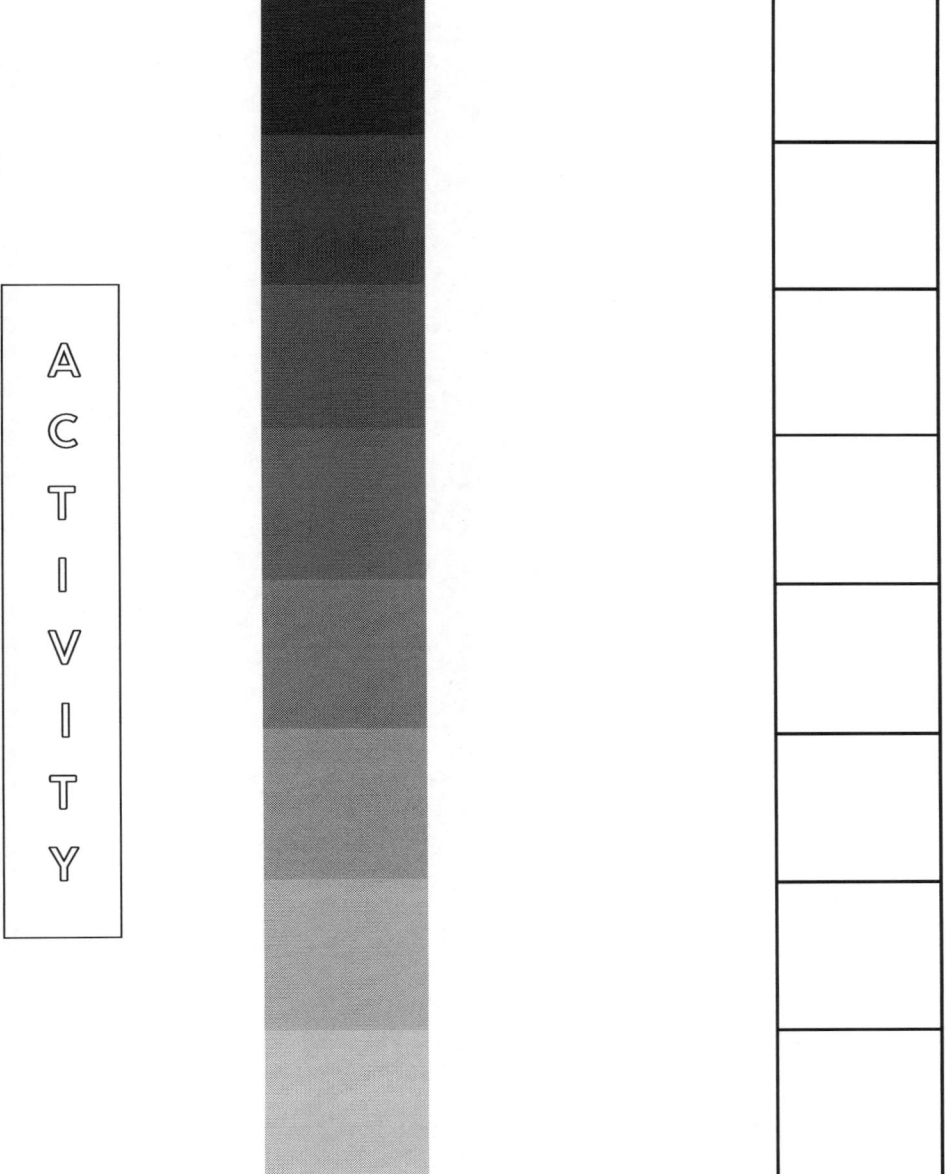

A
C
T
I
V
I
T
Y

color playlist

COLOR PICK

SONGS

KIRK FRANKLIN // "SOMETHING ABOUT THE NAME JESUS"

KRISTIAN STANFILL // "ONE THING REMAINS"

KORYN HAWTHORNE // "STAY AWAY"

KARI JOBE // "WHAT LOVE IS THIS"

YOUR PICK

SONGS

COLOR PICK

YOUTUBE

HEATHER LINDSEY // "RELATIONSHIPS: REFUSING TO SETTLE"

YOUR PICK

YOUTUBE

encouragement

Sis, maybe you've found
that you have been getting
comfortable with living a Gray
life, dating or talking to a Gray man,
or having a Gray relationship with God.
Well, today we're breaking up with Gray. It's
been here for too long, taken up too much of
your time, and caused you too much pain.
It's not always easy to break it off,
but I encourage you to ask our
Dad for help. He'll never
lead you astray.

prayers

chapter *feels*

_____

_____

_____

_____

_____

_____

_____

_____

_____

_____

_____

Okay, so did anybody else ever cry when their favorite TV characters broke up? It was just me? Sis, don't lie! I think I can (almost) confidently say that we all have. But why is it that we get so emotionally attached to characters who aren't even real? Why do we desire to have relationships that look like theirs, even if they're unhealthy? In this chapter, I told you about my not-so-wise plan to lose my virginity in order to gain love. Somewhere between bad relationships and media, I thought that sex was the only way I could earn a man's love. Well sis, if you have to earn love, the chances are that what you're "earning," isn't really love. But I know a Man who loves you without condition. Jesus. There's no way you could His love. He simply gives it to you, daily. So let Him love you back to life even if society is telling you something different. There's so much color waiting on the other side. So keep coloring, Queen. Keep on coloring.

social media madness

Social media can be a great tool for connecting with distant friends and family (and let's just be honest, those random people we follow too). Media sites allow the world to see you express yourself through art, videos, and photography. Social media is good for business and can even help spread the gospel but more often than not, we have taken this platform and used it as a means to make ourselves look good and compare ourselves against other people. Now more than ever, social media is being viewed as reality. We've traded in our fairytales TV show characters for the hottest celebrity couples, not realizing that all that glitters isn't gold. We're so invested in their lives that we want to live them. We want so-and-so to break up or we think they're cute and should stay together. Even with Christian couples, we always want a say in their business but neglect to take care of our own...

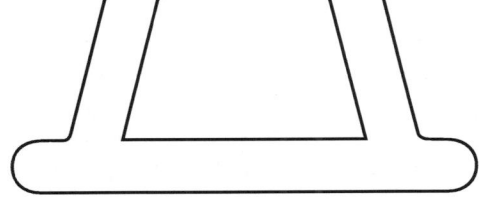

REFLECTION

How has social media shaped your idea of relationships?

After spending hours on social media sites, I found myself getting jealous. There were women with thousands of followers, who were beautiful, looked like they had it all together, and had (good-looking) boyfriends. They seemed perfect so I began to compare myself against them. **Have you ever compared yourself to other women? What did you gain/lose? How did it make you feel?**

Try to stay off of social media for 24 hours. That means no checking notifications, no posting, and no creeping. Use the time that you would normally spend on the sites to spend with God. **After the 24 hours is over, write down how you felt.**

I realize that some of you may not be lured in by the social media trap. **But what other areas of your life have caused you to be distracted from God?**

Who taught you how to love? What did you learn from them? Were you taught healthy or unhealthy behaviors? How has that affected your relationships (friendships, family, romantic) today?

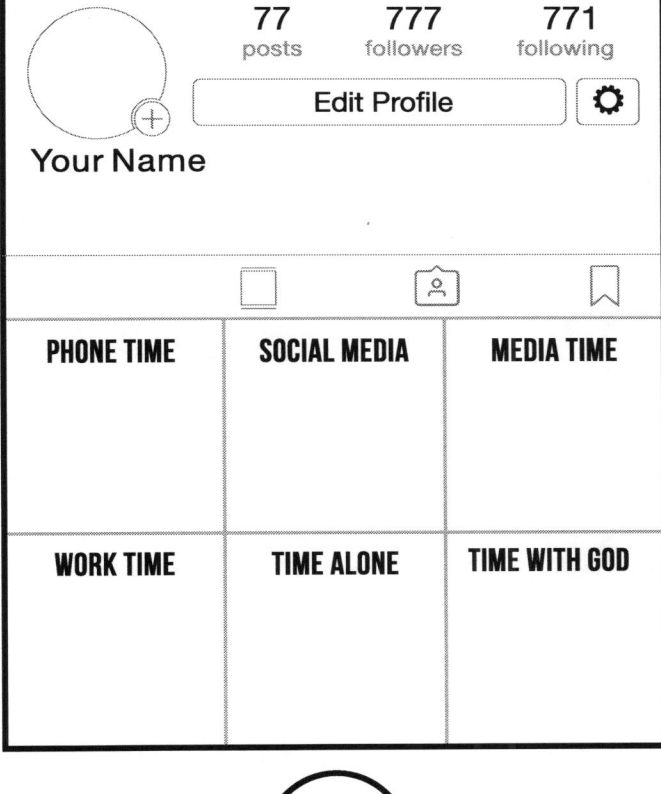

How are you spending your time?

1. Log how many hours you've spent on social media today.

2. Record how many hours you have consumed media today/talked about media (TV, internet, billboards, blogs, youtube, etc.)

3. Write down how much time you have spent with God today (i.e. prayers, reading, studying, worshipping, etc.) Compare how you've been spending your time today.

	77 posts	777 followers	771 following
	Edit Profile		⚙

Your Name

PHONE TIME	SOCIAL MEDIA	MEDIA TIME
WORK TIME	TIME ALONE	TIME WITH GOD

A C T I V I T Y

HAVE YOU BEEN PLUGGING IN OR RUNNING ON EMPTY? HAVE YOU BEEN PLUGGING IN OR RUNNING ON EMPTY? HAVE YOU BEEN PLUGGING IN OR RUNNING ON EMPTY?

color playlist

COLOR PICK

SONGS

CASS // WORTH FIGHTING FOR

MARIZU IKECHI // CHOSEN

DAVID & NICOLE BINION // HUNGER

MONTELL FISH // OVERCOME

YOUR PICK

SONGS

COLOR PICK

YOUTUBE

PASTOR MICHAEL TODD // EX IT SERIES

YOUR PICK

YOUTUBE

encouragement

Sis, you have been

called to a higher standard–

God's standard. Don't let society

lead you away from God and into the

arms of a Gray situation.

You are worth so

much more!

prayers

chapter *feels*

_____

_____

_____

_____

_____

_____

_____

_____

_____

_____

_____

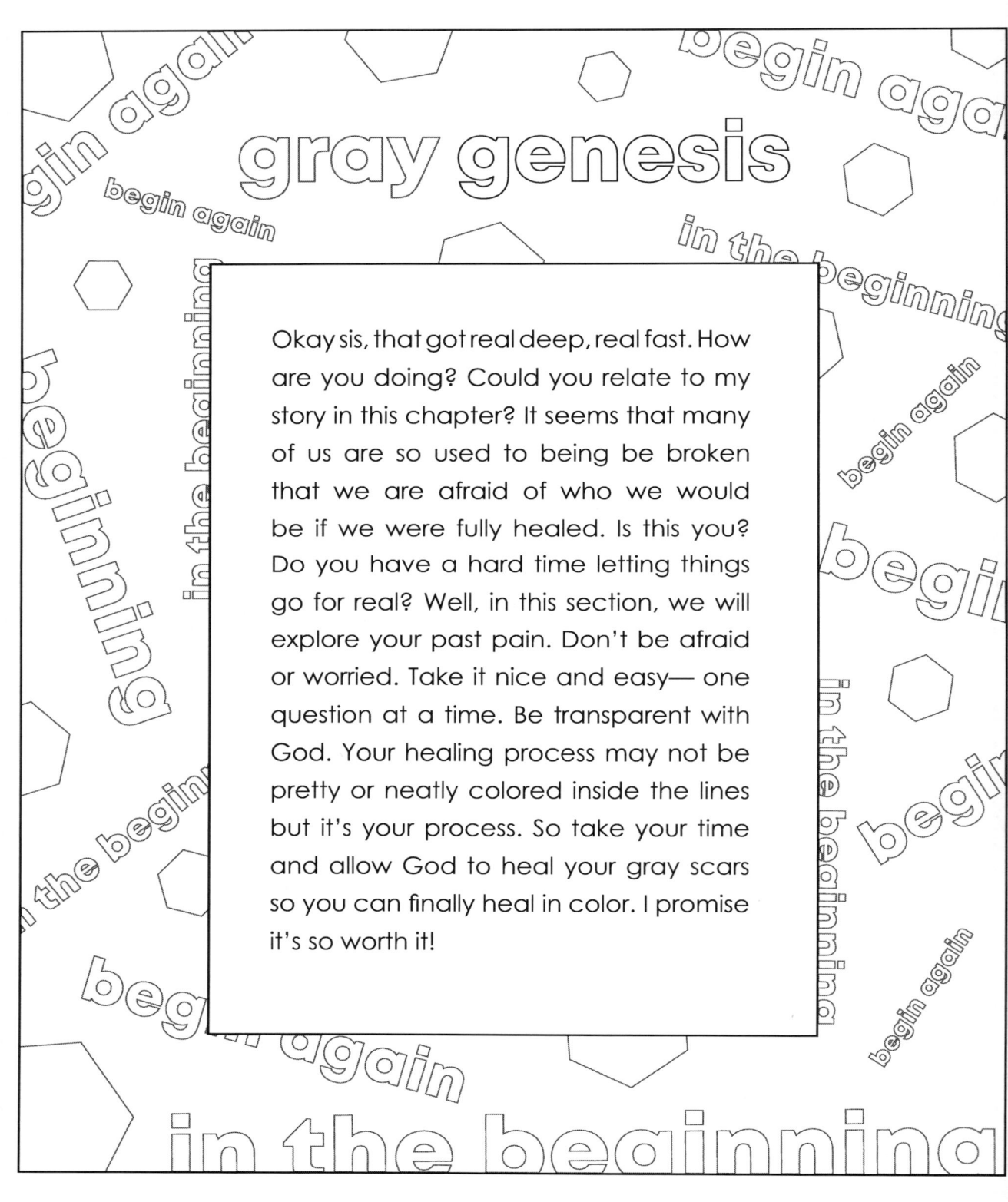

gray genesis

Okay sis, that got real deep, real fast. How are you doing? Could you relate to my story in this chapter? It seems that many of us are so used to being be broken that we are afraid of who we would be if we were fully healed. Is this you? Do you have a hard time letting things go for real? Well, in this section, we will explore your past pain. Don't be afraid or worried. Take it nice and easy— one question at a time. Be transparent with God. Your healing process may not be pretty or neatly colored inside the lines but it's your process. So take your time and allow God to heal your gray scars so you can finally heal in color. I promise it's so worth it!

a time to heal...

It's been said that "hurt people, hurt people" and I completely agree. When we forfeit proper healing and forgiveness that can only come through God, we open ourselves up to bitterness, shame, regret, feelings of worthlessness, and other tricks of the enemy. In this section, we will dig deep into your past: who hurt you, how you've carried the hurt around, and even how you have hurt others. Don't blow this off, sis. Be honest with yourself and bring all of your worries and fears to your Heavenly Father.

REFLECTION

What are the things in your life that you haven't healed from yet? What stopped you before? How will you try to fully heal this time?

Who have you hurt in your process of being unhealed? Have you forgiven yourself yet?

How do you plan on strengthening your relationship with God during this season of your life? List some practical ways that you can get closer to God each day.

Is God, alone, enough for you? Or do you feel like you need something/someone else to make you feel good? What do you use to fill your voids or hide your pain?

God's grace is so beautiful. It saves us daily and covers us continually. **Have you ever made a plan to sin and thought that it would be a better idea to ask God for forgiveness later? If so, think about that time and write it down. Now make a plan of how you will resist temptation in the future (see 1 Corinthians 10:13).**

Have you healed yet?

1. Write down the names of people who have hurt you in each circle. Draw more circles if needed.

2. Color the circles with the people you've forgiven in **green**.

3. Color the circles with the people you have not forgiven in **red**.

4. Write a prayer next to each red circle, asking for God's guidance in helping you forgive and heal from your past pain.

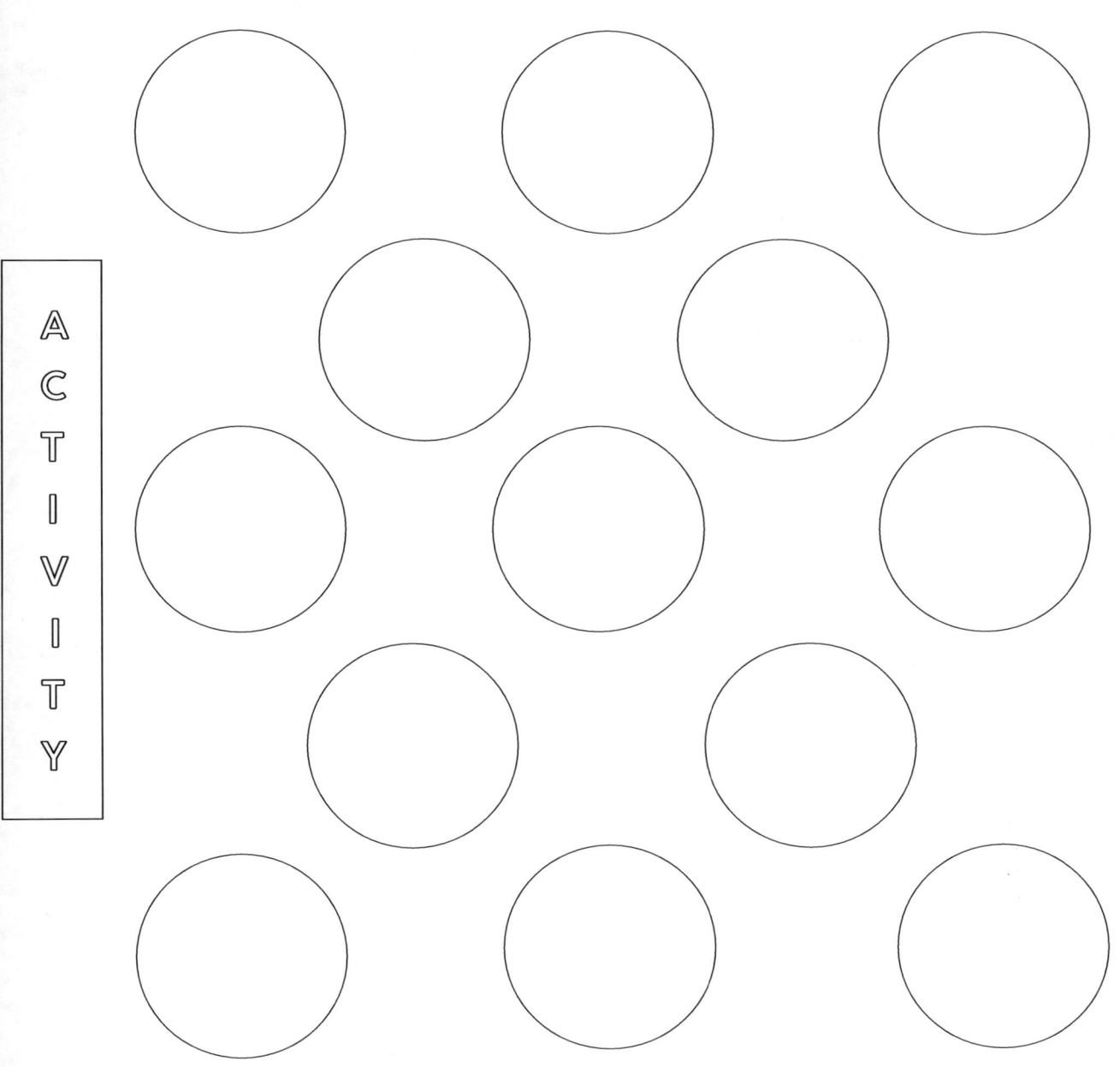

A
C
T
I
V
I
T
Y

color playlist

COLOR PICK

SONGS

HILLSONG UNITED // WHOLE HEART (HOLD ME NOW)

HILLSONG UNITED // EVEN WHEN IT HURTS (PRAISE SONG)

PSALMIST RAINE // THIS ALTAR (LIVE)

CALLEDOUT MUSIC // MY PRAYER (YAHWEH)

YOUR PICK

SONGS

COLOR PICK

YOUTUBE

PASTOR CHRISTINE CAINE // BROKEN PIECES

PASTOR MICHAEL TODD // DAMAGED GOODS SERIES

YOUR PICK

YOUTUBE

encouragement

Sis, there will always be things in life that cause us pain. In some cases, we may be the ones who cause ourselves hurt. If you've experienced any trauma, heartache, or pain, I'm pleading with you... Please hand that hurt over to Our Daddy. He wants his daughter back. He desires for you to have joy. Something beautiful can be birthed out of your pain. So don't give up on God and don't give up on yourself. All things WILL work together for your good! Keep fighting to live your life in color.

prayers

chapter *feels*

_____

_____

_____

_____

_____

_____

_____

_____

_____

_____

_____

dating gray

Hey sis, have you ever found yourself in a place where God was trying to pull you away from something or someone? He gave you all of the signs but you just weren't trying to hear it? Yeah, I've been there. But at some point, I got tired of repeating the same cycle. Are you tired yet, sis? We may know that God's plans for us are greater than our own. We may quote Jeremiah 29:11 all day but do we actually believe it? Do you believe that He'll come through for you or do you feel like you need to make your own plans? Well, in this section, we're going to cover what it means to seek God wholeheartedly, rushing ahead of God, dating Gray— I mean, bae, and God's plans for you. Are you ready? Don't quit on me, let's keep coloring!

are you thirsty?

Many times we reject what God wants us to do because our flesh is constantly waging war against our spirit. Still, it's up to us to decide who will win (hint: choose your spirit). It's up to us to decide if we want to stop being so-- Thirsty. Yes, sis. Thirsty. Our Heavenly Father desires to grow closer to us and supply us with Living Water. Still, sometimes we'd rather settle for anything that can quench our thirst at the moment. We have all been the woman at the well before, but today, I'm challenging you to accept the Living Water and desire to seek God rather than your boo. Boo's come and go. Some will even get ghost on you (Please forgive the corny nature of that joke. I just had to do it). But seriously, the time has come for you to stop playing with God and hand Him the thing or person who's keeping you away from a genuine relationship with Him. So leave Casper alone and start living your life in color!

REFLECTION

Have you ever found yourself trying to rush ahead of God? How did that work out for you? In what ways did that decision affect your life, even now? If you could relive that situation, what would you do differently?

How have you been seeking God wholeheartedly? If you haven't, in what ways could you improve?

This question requires some serious honesty. Are you dating someone right now? Has God given you permission to be with the guy? If not, why are you still trying to hold onto your situationship?

Jesus replied, "if you only knew the gift God has for you and who you are speaking to, you would ask me, and I would give you living water." (John 4:10) Sometimes we don't know the gifts that God has for us or how much He loves us because we are too preoccupied in our attempt to gain love and affection from other people. **Think about your life and write down the things that God has been trying to show you but you've continued to ignore.**

Read John 4:11-12. In these verses, the Samaritan woman had ALL the excuses: "You don't have... Where? How?" Sounds like some of us, huh? Well, I've had plenty of these moments with God. "God, how are you going to... How am I going to recover from this breakup? Who else will be with me? Why won't you let me..." We can get pretty full of questions sometimes. **Have you been questioning God lately? Have you waited for His response or did your questions turn into complaints?**

#THIRSTY

1. Read John 4 in three different translations (my faves are the New Living Translation (NLT), the English Standard Version (ESV), The Message (MSG), and The Amplified (AMP)

2. Picture yourself as the Samaritan woman. On the outside of the cup, write down the ways that you relate to her.

3. Inside the cup, write the areas of your life that you've been thirsty in. After you write inside the cup, color it **dark blue** (sapphire in color code guide), representing washing and cleansing.

A
C
T
I
V
I
T
Y

color playlist

COLOR PICK

SONGS

MARVIN SAPP // THIRSTY

KORYN HAWTHORNE // STAY AWAY

SARAH REEVES // NOWHERE

RAY JUNE // GOOD THING (SOUNDCLOUD)

YOUR PICK

SONGS

COLOR PICK

YOUTUBE

PASTOR MICHAEL TODD // THE MYTH OF DATING :: RELATIONSHIP GOALS

PASTOR STEVEN FURTICK // WHAT'S BLOCKING YOUR BREAKTHROUGH?

HEATHER LINDSEY // DEAL-BREAKERS BEFORE THE RING

PASTOR STEVEN FURTICK // THE THIRST TRAP

PASTOR MICHAEL TODD // THIRST TRAP

YOUR PICK

YOUTUBE

encouragement

Sis, if you are dating someone who you KNOW is not God's best for you, if you aren't God's best for the guy right now, or if you're spending more time with bae and literally putting him "before anyone else," including God, take it from someone who's been there (time and time again), leave that man alone! God wants to do something amazing through you but if you don't even have a relationship with Him, you will block your blessing. Breakups are hard but disobedience will cost you so much more. Don't be fearful of being alone, instead, be content with God and God alone. Learn how to love Him before you get blindsided by the world's ideas of love. He'll love you back to life.

prayers

chapter *feels*

LOOK!

I STAND AT THE DOOR AND KNOCK. IF YOU HEAR MY VOICE AND OPEN THE DOOR, I WILL COME IN, AND WE WILL SHARE A MEAL TOGETHER AS FRIENDS.

-REVELATION 3:20

gray dates

Welcome Queen, you made it to the dinner table! The waiter is about to come and take your order. Have you figured out what you want to eat yet? Do you want nourishment for your spirit or a quick fix for your emptiness? Many times, we can find ourselves lacking nutrients (a relationship) from God because we do not consistently take the time to be fed by Him. So we spiritually stuff ourselves with unhealthy relationships instead of patiently preparing a healthy relationship with Our Father, ourselves, and then others. As our hunger increases, we become desperate to eat as soon as possible (sometimes attitudes are involved and we get "hangry" but we'll keep that between us) then essentially settle for fast food in our relationships... Okay, the waiter is here and you've been waiting to eat for a while now! What are you going to order: greasy, fried food that lacks color and nutrients or a meal that includes an array of colors and will not only satisfy your hunger but your body's needs? It's up to you, sis. What will you have for dinner tonight?

appetite

As a child, I loved being in the kitchen when my granny used to bake her mouth-watering desserts. It was like I had a natural inclination for all things buttery and sugary. After she would finish mixing the cake or brownie batter, she always let lick the bowl (this was before the warnings about eating raw eggs were publicized). I almost enjoyed the batter more than the cake itself. Even though I know the potential food-borne illnesses that can arise from eating raw eggs as well as the chronic diseases that can come along with over-indulging in desserts, I'm still drawn to them... Can I eat cake batter and cookie dough? Of course I can! I'm a grown woman. But is it beneficial or even wise to do? Nah, not so much...

REFLECTION

What areas of your life are you neglecting wisdom from the Holy Spirit (the Bible, godly people, etc.) and continuing to entertain your unhealthy habits?

Many times we crave what we are used to feeding ourselves. For instance, I find myself craving more and more sugar as I continue to eat dessert on a regular basis. When I eat healthily, I crave more healthy foods.

Sometimes, people in my life will try to hold me accountable for what I put into my body. **Who do you have in your life right now that is trying to keep you healthy? Are you rejecting their advice and getting mad when they tell you about your unhealthy habits? Why or why not?**

Have you allowed God into your heart yet? Does He have a seat at your dinner table or the seat taken by another man? Are you afraid of being alone with Your Father?

What have you been feeding yourself spiritually? Has it been unicolored, unhealthy meals that will harm you (i.e. gossip, lying, cheating, sleeping around, degrading music, trash TV, bad friends, etc.)?

What healthy meals have you been eating lately (i.e. reading the Bible, spending time with God, listening to sermons, having godly community/ friends that will hold you accountable for your actions, praying, going to church, working on areas of your life that you're struggling in, etc)? Are you consistent with your eating habits?

Microwave

What areas of your life have you tried to get quick results as a substitute to fill your voids, rather than waiting on God's direction?

1. Write those areas inside of the microwave.

2. Inside the mixing bowls, write down the areas of your life that you need to spend more time allowing God to prepare you.

3. Under "ingredients," write down the characteristics you need in order to confront and conquer those areas (3 have been listed to start you off).

4. Under "directions," write down the direction that you've received from God so far.

A
C
T
I
V
I
T
Y

12:00AM

① ② ③
④ ⑤ ⑥
⑦ ⑧ ⑨
START ⓪ STOP

recipe

INGREDIENTS:
trust, faith, patience,

DIRECTIONS:

color playlist

COLOR PICK

SONGS

TAMELA MANN // CHANGE ME

STEFANY GRETZINGER // CONFIDENT

GAWVI // FIGHT FOR ME

JONATHAN MCREYNOLDS // MAKE ROOM

YOUR PICK

SONGS

COLOR PICK

YOUTUBE

HEATHER LINDSEY // GOD TOLD ME HE WAS THE ONE

KIERRA SHEARD // HOW TO: GET OVER IT

SARAH JAKES ROBERTS // BEGIN AGAIN

HEATHER LINDSEY // SWEET TOOTH

YOUR PICK

YOUTUBE

encouragement

Beautiful sister, you are so loved! Like, for real. You are loved! I know how easy it can be to fall into the trap of feeling worthless, or thinking that you're not enough or not worthy to be fully loved by God. I know that sometimes, you may have your doubts. You may not think that God can take your bad cravings away. I get it, for real. But He will bring you out if you do the real work of letting Him in and being transparent. He already knows you. You can't hide from Him. So invite Him into your heart— to your dinner table, and share a meal with Our Father so He can love you back to life.

prayers

chapter *feels*

_____

_____

_____

_____

_____

_____

_____

_____

_____

_____

_____

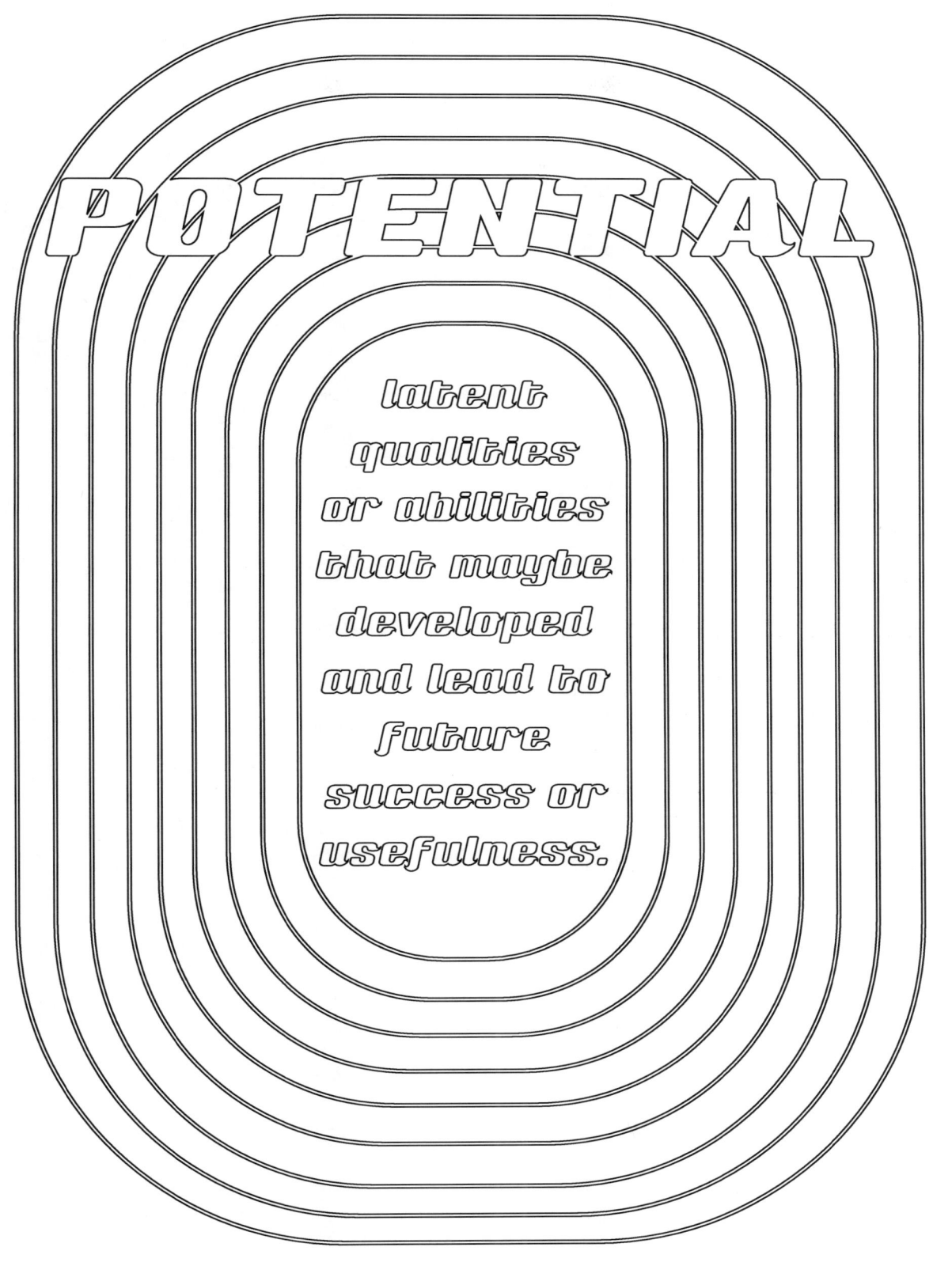

POTENTIAL

latent
qualities
or abilities
that maybe
developed
and lead to
future
success or
usefulness.

gray potential

Sister! How are you feeling after reading this? Have you ever been guilty of staying with someone for their potential and not for who they truly were? Well, this chapter really, really hit home for me. I know, I wrote the whole book. So it all hits home but this, right here... Listen, sis, falling for potential can be so dangerous. I know that seeing people for who they are can be difficult, especially if you're emotionally attached to them. I remember a time when I used to pray for guys like this, "Lord, please just help him love you more," which wasn't a bad prayer but my perspective off. I was trying to rearrange God's plan and ignore the fact that His son had not yet established a relationship with Him. I wanted someone who didn't know God personally, to love me completely. That is impossible because the man's inability to love and know God meant that he could not fully know or love himself. If he didn't know or love himself, then there was no way that he could possibly love me. This doesn't mean that the guy was a bad person, he just wasn't who God had for me. The same holds true for you. God has better for you but if you are focused on fixing someone else (even through prayer), then you cannot allow Our Father to fix and prepare YOU for His best. So open your eyes to see beyond the gray areas of potential and start viewing the world in color.

discipline

I played sports in high school, so I know what it's like to be trained. Although I was never the most talented player, I always desired to be the most disciplined one. Still, my desire for discipline did not leave the parameters of the court or the track. In many ways, I wanted to be more disciplined in sports than I wanted to be in my relationship with God. My body was in shape, but my spirit was so unhealthy. Because I lacked discipline, it showed up in various areas of my life, including my relationships. I would always focus on the potential of the guy I was dating and ignore the calling that God placed on my life...

REFLECTION

How has God coached you through life? What direction has he given you so far?

What kind of player have you been? Have you been lazy, disciplined, eager to learn and take direction, or annoyed that the Coach is making you work?

What plans have you had that you tried to make God fit into because you wanted full control? What scares you about letting God have complete control over your life?

Have you ever allowed yourself to be in a dysfunctional relationship? Were you focused on the person's potential rather than who they showed themselves to be? What was the outcome of that relationship? How did you recognize that they weren't God's best for you? Are you constantly trying to rekindle that old relationship for fear of being alone?

Are you afraid of being single? If so, what caused that fear? Was it society? Your parents or lack of parents? Friends or family? Social media? Your favorite show, etc? Who or what taught you how to be scared of singleness?

Are you a fixer? Have you ever been able to fully transform any man that you have been with? Are you only attracted to men who you think you can fix? Does trying to "fix" other people make you feel secure in your own dysfunction?

What is God trying to develop in you that you haven't been practicing for? What has kept you from practicing consistently? How much do you think your development is worth and how much have you invested in it? Are your relationships cultivating your spiritual growth or stunting it?

GOD'S PLAN

If you've ever driven by any massive building, you may have marveled at its size, architecture, or maybe just its overall dope-ness (yes, I made that word up). Still, no building, great or small, could ever be built without a well-thought-out blueprint. Blueprints essentially show the potential of a piece of land or property. They are the roadmap that helps the builder create something out of nothing. As believers, we must realize that God already has the blueprint for our lives. He has the plan for our ultimate success (Jeremiah 29:11). However, we've all tried to add our own suggestions to His perfect plan. When we don't like the paint color He picks out, are annoyed by the materials He uses, or think that so-and-so's building looks better than ours, we try to remodel what hasn't been fully developed yet. Maybe this is why we feel incomplete sometimes. We'd rather make our own plans than follow God's blueprint...

1. Read the scriptures listed below and color **Blueprint A&B** according to what took place (Genesis 1:26-31, 2:1-25 & Genesis 3).

2. Study the themes of these scriptures (i.e. Creation, The Fall, Redemption, Restoration, etc.)

3. In **Blueprint C**, write down the falls that have made the greatest impact on your life.

4. In **Blueprint D**, write down God's ultimate plan for you. Find Biblical references to back it up (ex. "I am fully taken care of. Psalm 23")

5. Think about how all of these things are interconnected. Ask God for revelation and strategy that will help you stay committed to **His plan** rather than your own.

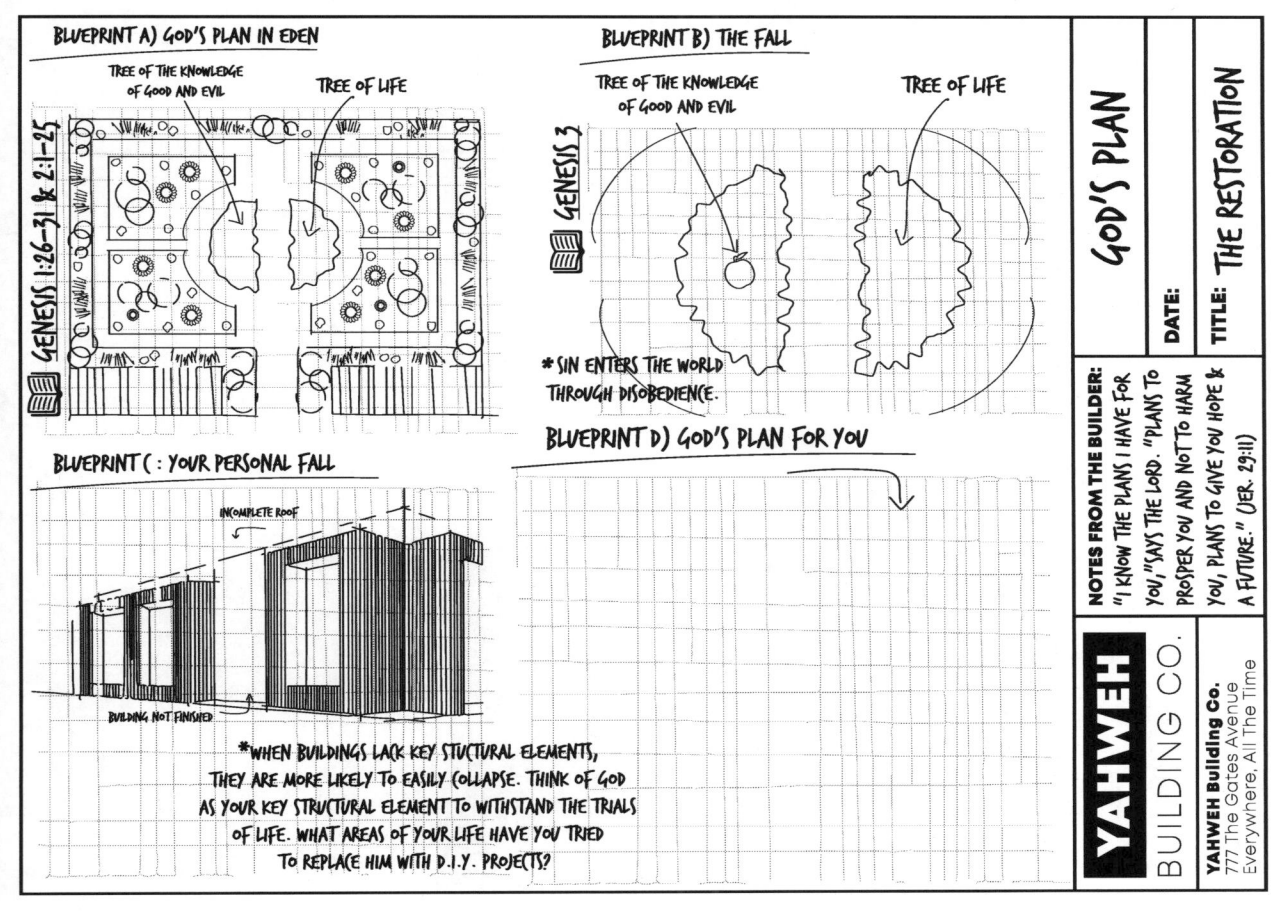

BLUEPRINT A) GOD'S PLAN IN EDEN

GENESIS 1:26-31 & 2:1-25

TREE OF THE KNOWLEDGE OF GOOD AND EVIL

TREE OF LIFE

BLUEPRINT B) THE FALL

GENESIS 3

TREE OF THE KNOWLEDGE OF GOOD AND EVIL

TREE OF LIFE

*SIN ENTERS THE WORLD THROUGH DISOBEDIENCE.

BLUEPRINT C: YOUR PERSONAL FALL

INCOMPLETE ROOF

BUILDING NOT FINISHED

*WHEN BUILDINGS LACK KEY STUCTURAL ELEMENTS, THEY ARE MORE LIKELY TO EASILY COLLAPSE. THINK OF GOD AS YOUR KEY STRUCTURAL ELEMENT TO WITHSTAND THE TRIALS OF LIFE. WHAT AREAS OF YOUR LIFE HAVE YOU TRIED TO REPLACE HIM WITH D.I.Y. PROJECTS?

BLUEPRINT D) GOD'S PLAN FOR YOU

GOD'S PLAN

DATE:

TITLE: THE RESTORATION

NOTES FROM THE BUILDER: "I KNOW THE PLANS I HAVE FOR YOU," SAYS THE LORD. "PLANS TO PROSPER YOU AND NOT TO HARM YOU, PLANS TO GIVE YOU HOPE & A FUTURE." (JER. 29:11)

YAHWEH BUILDING CO.

YAHWEH Building Co.
777 The Gates Avenue
Everywhere, All The Time

color playlist

COLOR PICK

SONGS

THE WALLS GROUP // THE PRAYER

LAUREN DAIGLE // ONCE AND FOR ALL

SARAH REEVES // EASY

TRAVIS GREENE // WHILE I'M WAITING

YOUR PICK

SONGS

COLOR PICK

YOUTUBE

HEATHER LINDSEY // UNEQUALLY YOKED RELATIONSHIPS (9MIN)

KIERRA SHEARD // HOW TO: BE SINGLE IN CUFFING SEASON

PASTOR SARAH JAKES ROBERTS // MAKE YOUR BED

PASTOR STEVEN FURTICK // CHOOSE YOUR CHAINS

YOUR PICK

YOUTUBE

encouragement

Beautiful Queen, God absolutely adores you. He didn't make any mistakes when He made you! Sometimes we can fall into bad habits that lead us down our own path, rather than Our Father's plan. Still, He wants the best for you. His plans are better than yours. His thoughts are higher. He can see you beyond your situation and He desires for you to seek Him so that you can be fulfilled. So let God coach you into greatness as He reveals His colorful plans to you!

prayers

chapter *feels*

_____

_____

_____

_____

_____

_____

_____

_____

_____

_____

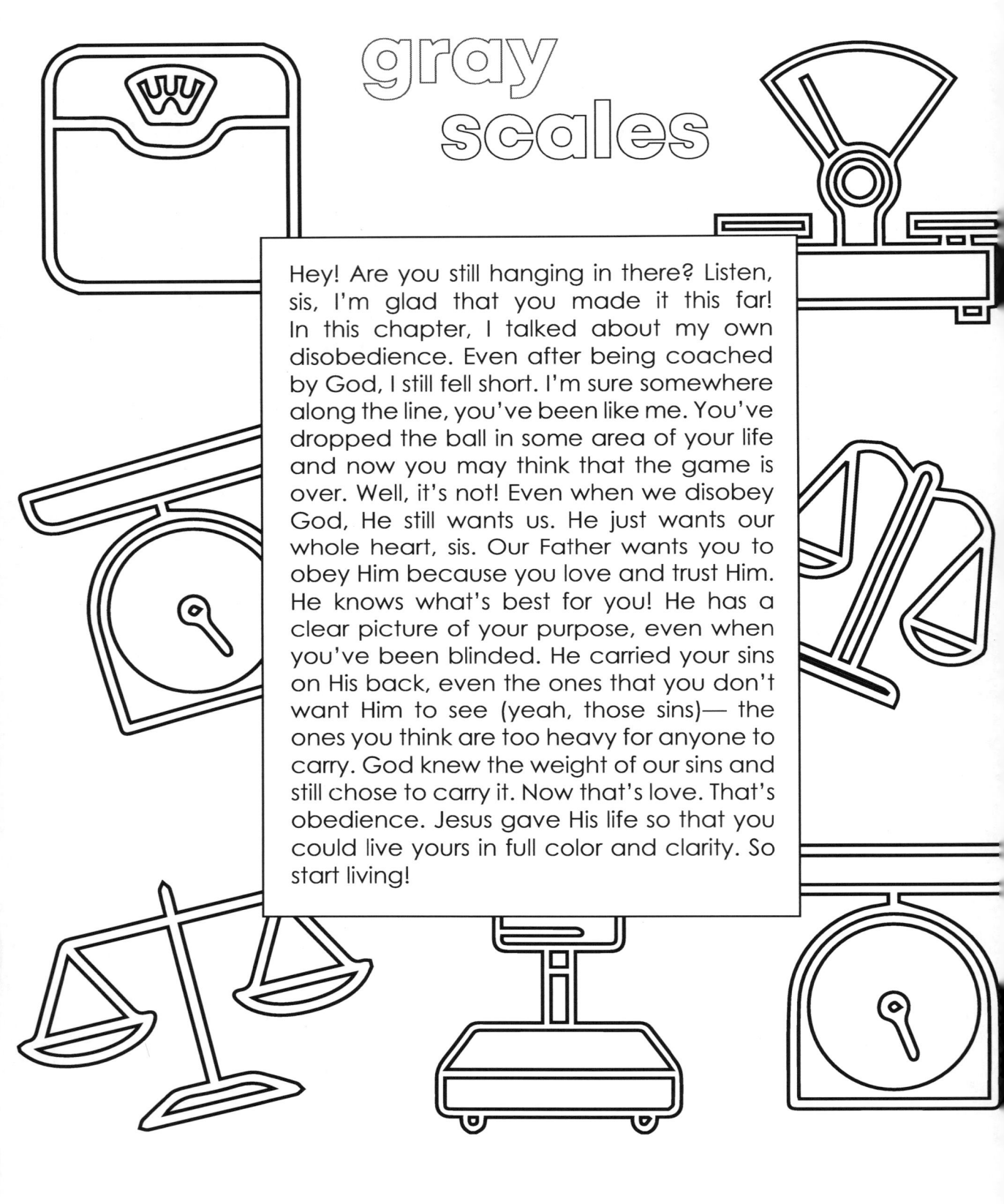

Hey! Are you still hanging in there? Listen, sis, I'm glad that you made it this far! In this chapter, I talked about my own disobedience. Even after being coached by God, I still fell short. I'm sure somewhere along the line, you've been like me. You've dropped the ball in some area of your life and now you may think that the game is over. Well, it's not! Even when we disobey God, He still wants us. He just wants our whole heart, sis. Our Father wants you to obey Him because you love and trust Him. He knows what's best for you! He has a clear picture of your purpose, even when you've been blinded. He carried your sins on His back, even the ones that you don't want Him to see (yeah, those sins)— the ones you think are too heavy for anyone to carry. God knew the weight of our sins and still chose to carry it. Now that's love. That's obedience. Jesus gave His life so that you could live yours in full color and clarity. So start living!

blinded

But the Lord said, "Go, for Saul is my chosen instrument to take my message to the Gentiles and to kings, as well as to the people of Israel. And I will show him how much he must suffer for my name's sake." So Ananias went and found Saul. He laid his hands on him and said, "Brother Saul, the Lord Jesus, who appeared to you on the road, has sent me so that you might regain your sight and be filled with the Holy Spirit." Instantly something like scales fell from Saul's eyes, and he regained his sight. Then he got up and was baptized. (Acts 9:15-18) If you know anything about Saul, you know that he hated Christians to the point that he would murder them. It wasn't until Jesus blinded Saul, that he was finally able to see the error in his ways. Even though Saul did horrible things, God still chose him, changed his name, healed his eyes, and allowed him to walk in the fullness of his purpose. So no matter what you've done in your past, just know that God is still choosing you. He will restore your vision and allow you to walk in a beautiful relationship with Him. He's just waiting on you to choose Him too…

REFLECTION

Has there ever been a time when you claimed that you were "blinded by love?" After reading this chapter, how do you feel about the saying, "blinded by love?"

Loving God requires that you submit your plans to Him. Your obedience is the key to unlock the fullness of your breakthrough. **What has God been requiring of you that you have not done yet?**

Have you allowed God to remove the scales from your eyes yet? Or are you still trying to navigate the world blindly? Why or why not?

Read all of Acts 9 and take notes here.

In the chapter, you will find that Ananias (who God sent to Saul) fit the qualifications of someone whom Saul would have killed in his past. In fact, Ananias was scared to help Saul at first. However, he finally obeyed God's instruction. Our obedience to God extends past the boundaries of our own lives. When God tells us to do something, it's not just for our own benefit, but the benefit of others. **With this in mind, who has your obedience (to God) helped? Who has your disobedience hurt? You may not know who your obedience/ disobedience will potentially affect. So also include the individuals that your decisions could affect.**

Weighed Priorities

1. Write down all of your current responsibilities in the box, below the scale.

2. On the lines to the right of the scale, rank the order that you tend to your priorities

(i.e. Taking care of my family, 2. Paying bills, 3. Getting through school, etc.)

3. Now list your high-priority items inside the low side of the scale.

4. List your lower-priority items inside the high side of the scale.

5. Where did God rank on your list?

priorities.

_____

_____

_____

_____

_____

_____

_____

_____

_____

responsibilities.

color playlist

COLOR PICK

RAY JUNE // SAME OL' SONG

HILLSONG UNITED // BROKEN VESSELS (AMAZING GRACE)

MONTELL FISH // WHATEVER YOU WANT

STEFANY GRETZINGER // LETTING GO

MONTELL FISH // CLEAR PICTURE

S O N G S

YOUR PICK

S O N G S

COLOR PICK

HEATHER LINDSEY // I CAN'T LET GO OF MY LIFE & TRUST GOD

PASTOR SARAH JAKES ROBERTS // EVERYTHING MUST GO

JOSEPH SOLOMON // AM I A LUKEWARM CHRISTIAN

PASTOR STEVEN FURTICK // DRAINED

Y O U T U B E

YOUR PICK

Y O U T U B E

encouragement

There is hope for you, sister!
Believe that God is Who He says
He is. He gave His only Son for you.
He wants His absolute best for you. He is
your Heavenly Father. God will always take
care of you. This is what you have to believe in
order to regain your sight. Believe that God will
heal you. He will restore those hidden things inside
of you that no one else knows about. Our Daddy
sees you. But you have to work too. You must
believe that He will remove the scales from
your eyes and allow you to see again,
this time, in full color. Just
believe, sis. Just believe...

prayers

chapter *feels*

_____

_____

_____

_____

_____

_____

_____

_____

_____

_____

_____

gray idols

How are you feeling, sis? In this chapter, I wrote about the difficulties that I experienced while trying to deepen my relationship with God and balance my hectic life. I failed miserably at times. It seems that just about everything I did took precedence over Him and spiritually, I suffered for it. What about you? How have you been managing your life? Have you allowed busyness to rule you? Has your calendar been your lord? Well, in this section, we're going to look a little closer at the things that have taken God's place in your life. It doesn't have to be a romantic relationship. It can be school, work, or even different ministries. ANYTHING you place above God is an idol. So let's start tearing those gray idols down so that you can submit your life to God and finally live in color!

seek first

But seek first his kingdom and his righteousness, and all these things will be given to you as well. Therefore do not worry about tomorrow, for tomorrow will worry about itself. Each day has enough trouble of its own.

Matthew 6:33-34 (New International Version)

Have you been putting God first in your life? If so, how have you been doing it? If not, what are some practical ways that you can put Him first every day? How can you deepen your relationship with Your Father in this season of your life?

Have you ever been impatient with God? If so, what caused you to be impatient? What were you waiting on Him for?

What have you tried to fill the voids in your life with other than God? Did you realize that you were making those things into idols?

Who or what do you trust more than God? It could be your finances, your bae, your job, your education, or even your pastor. Who is the first person or thing that you go to when you need help? Who is the first person you speak to in the morning? What is the first thing that you do when you wake up? If you pay attention, your routines and schedules will show you who you worship/serve consistently.

Have you ever recognized that you were becoming someone else's idol? If so, how did you handle the situation?

Watch The Throne

Every day, there will be countless things that try to (subtly) take your focus off of your Heavenly Father. As you slowly shift your focus from God, all of these things can become idols in your life. It's up to you to dethrone anything that begins to take the place of God. That doesn't mean kick everyone out of your life. It just means that you have to put everything in its proper place. (If it's not pleasing to God, you should definitely cut yourself off from it) So what will have to fall off so that God can take His rightful place in your heart?

1. Color the main throne according to the labels within the image.
2. In the small chairs, write down the things/people that have taken the throne of your heart.
3. Inside the stairs, write a prayer to God as you dethrone everything that has stood in the way of your relationship with Him. Ask for forgiveness and make up in your mind that you will seek Him above all else.

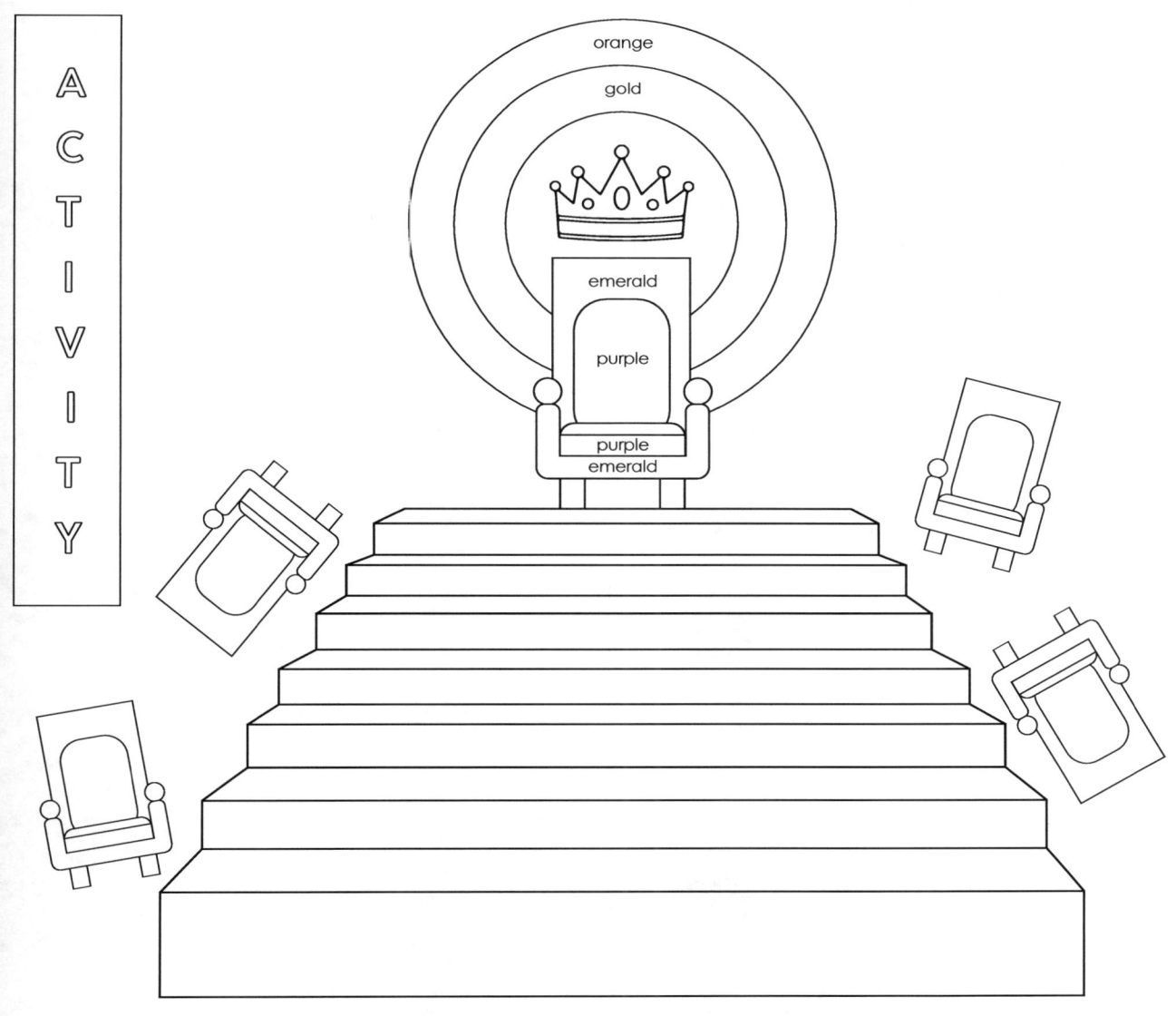

color playlist

COLOR PICK

SONGS

GIL JOE X NKAY // SHACKLES

WYLD // TO BE NEAR YOU

SEU WORSHIP // BREATHE

SHEKINAH GLORY // YES

PSALMIST RAINE // I SURRENDER

YOUR PICK

SONGS

COLOR PICK

YOUTUBE

PASTOR MIKE TODD // 24EVER SERIES

PASTOR MIKE TODD // RELEASE (STOP HOLDING IT)

PASTOR STEVEN FURTICK // COME THROUGH DRIPPIN'

YOUR PICK

YOUTUBE

encouragement

Sis, I don't want you to feel guilty if you've had idols pop up in your life. We've all had them. In fact, each day, there will be a million opportunities to choose those idols above God. The key is to recognize when your focus is shifting. Ask God to make your spirit sensitive to Him. When you begin to worship other things with your time, thoughts, and outward expressions ask God to lead you back to Him. He's faithful and He's waiting on you to dethrone everything that's taking up His space in your heart. Once you do, He will lead you back to His heart so that you can live your life in color!

prayers

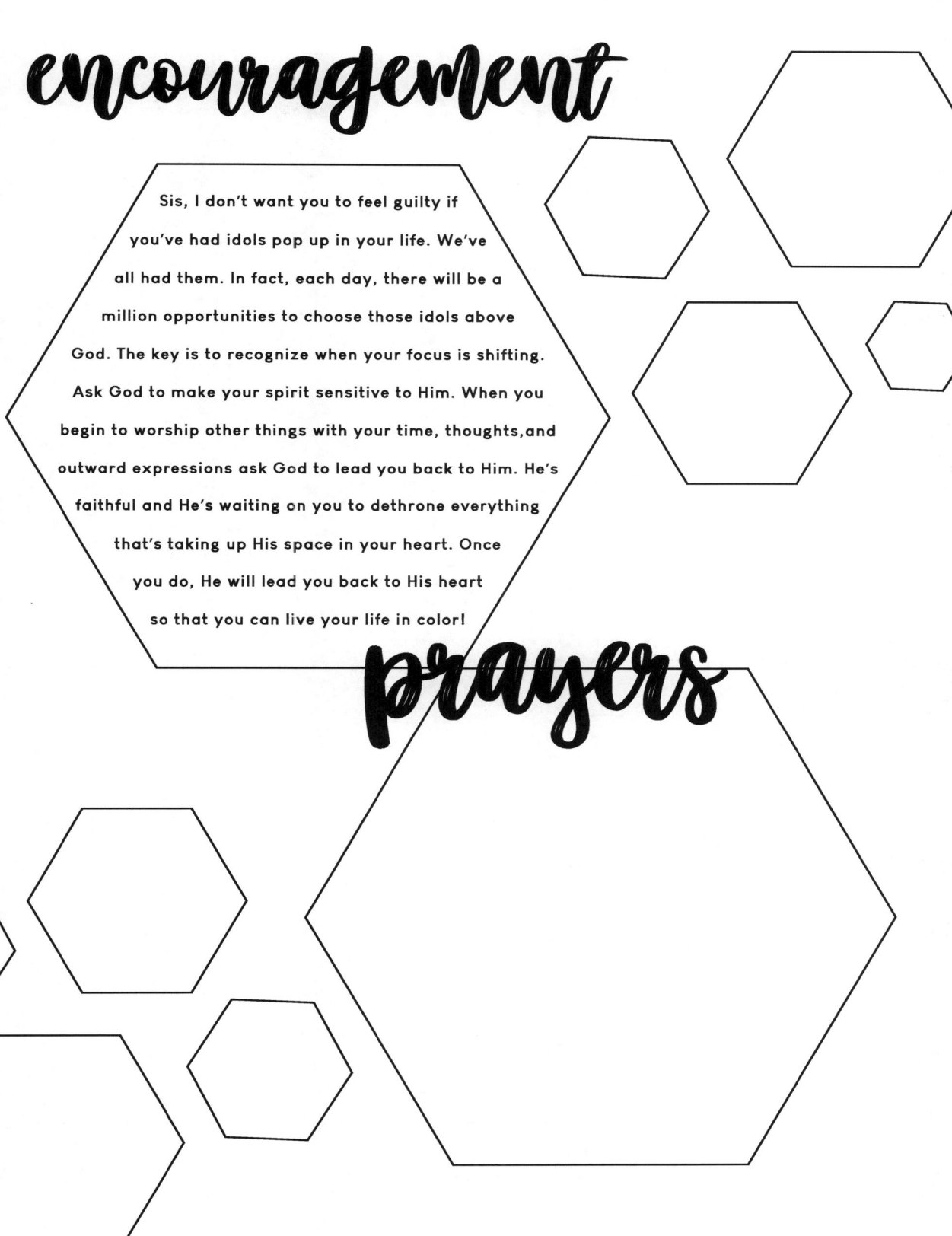

chapter *feels*

_____

_____

_____

_____

_____

_____

_____

_____

_____

_____

Guard your heart above all else, for it determines the course of your life.

proverbs 4:23

gray-zoned

Sis! Welcome back! I'm so proud of you for making it this far. So how are you feeling? Could you relate to this chapter? I began the chapter by defining "excuses" because that's exactly what the gray-zone is: an excuse. I know I wrote a lot about my experience (being gray-zoned) but I only touched a little bit on how we can gray-zone Our Father. Have you ever been guilty of putting God in the gray-zone then trying to give the excuse, "well God knows my heart" to make yourself look or feel better? We've all been guilty of doing this in some way, but the truth is that God does know our hearts and He loves us regardless of the mess that's going on inside of them. So it's time for us to drop our excuses when it comes to Our Daddy. He knows us better than we know ourselves. When we keep it real with God, we allow him to heal the hidden areas that no one else knows about. So, Queen, the choice is yours. Are you ready to start keeping it 100? Well then, let's keep coloring!

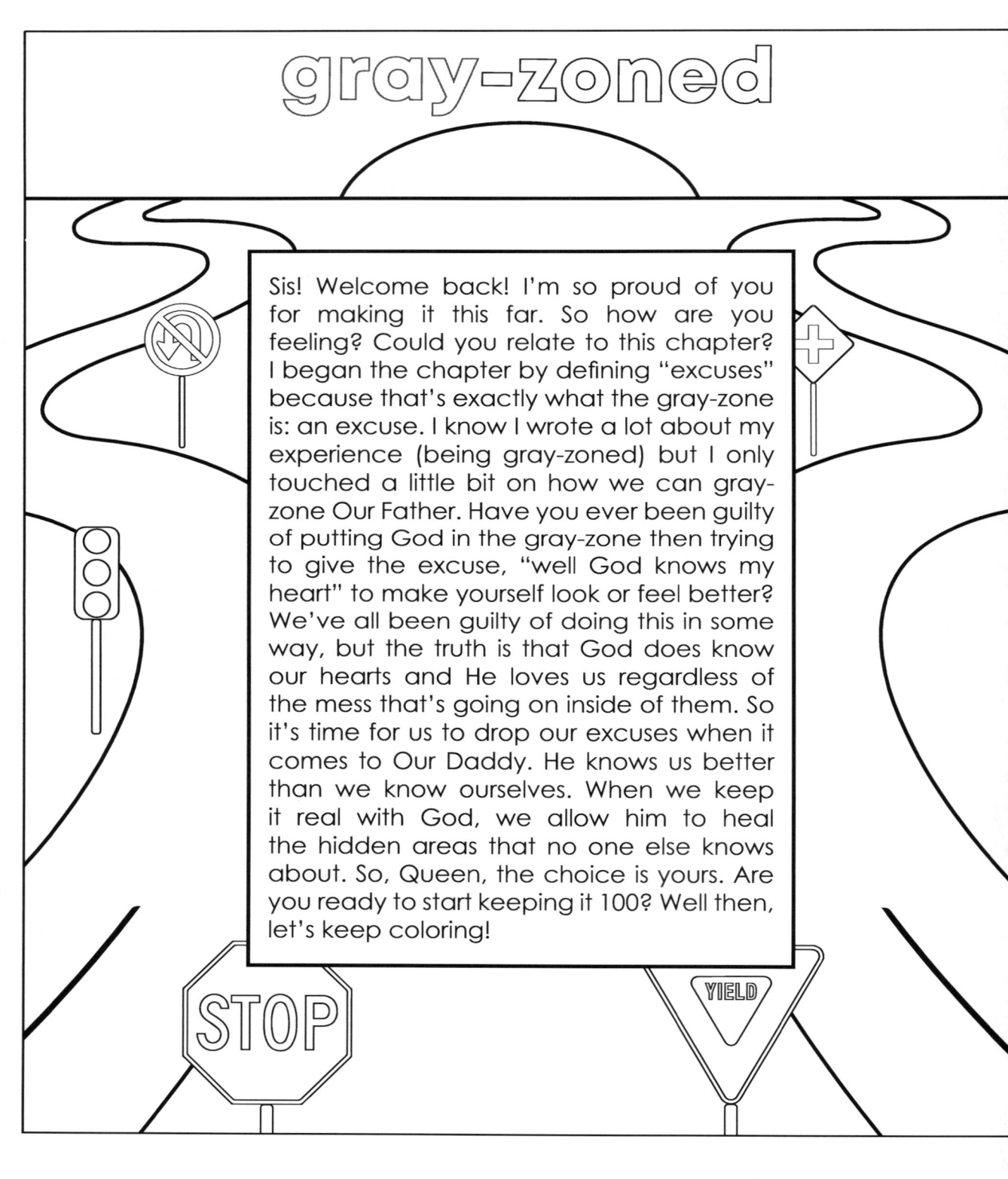

what are excuses?

"My child, pay attention to what I say. Listen carefully to my words. Don't lose sight of them. Let them penetrate deep into your heart, for they bring life to those who find them, and healing to their whole body. Guard your heart above all else, for it determines the course of your life." **Proverbs 4:20-23**

You may have heard or seen this verse a million times before. You may have never seen it. But today, I am challenging you to take it seriously. In our culture, there is such an abundance of things that our minds can be loaded with. There are countless forms of media all around us, advertisements, music, television, and much more. All of these things want your attention but you have the power to choose what you want to pay attention to. Because ultimately, you are paying something to take it all in, whether it's your time or your peace. There's always an exchange. So today, I want you to choose God. Choose His peace so that He can bring you into the fullness of His colorful plan for your life.

REFLECTION

When was the last time that you made an excuse? What was it? Why did you decide to make an excuse instead of taking full responsibility? Who taught you that excuses were permissible?

Have you ever been on the other side of an excuse? Did you believe the excuse that the person gave? What made you believe or not believe them?

How have excuses affected the totality of your relationships (not just romantic)? Have they caused resentment? Have you ever noticed the number of excuses that were present (whether from you or the other person)? What steps can you take in order to get rid of the excuses in your life?

Have you ever asked the famous question, "what are we doing?" What made you ask the question? Did you already know where the situation was headed? If so, why did you desire to hang onto the situationship?

What's your gray-zone story? Have you been the person who doesn't want to be committed at any point? How did you take on that role? Have you been the person who left the "what are we doing?" conversation heartbroken? What steps did you take to heal from that situation? If you haven't healed fully, write down an action plan to address it and take it to God.

Zone Defense

Teams sometimes use a zone defense to ensure that there aren't any players from the opposing team left open to score. The five players are designated an area on the court to guard. The circles represent you. The goal (with the heart in it) represents your heart. The squares represent the opposing team (things that will potentially harm you). The opposing team wants your heart, but you have to guard it at all costs.

1. What areas of your life do you need to be more intentional about guarding your heart? (i.e. friends, family, negative people, gossip, jealousy, greed, selfishness, lust, abusive relationships, music, TV, etc.) Which opposing team has scored so far? Write these things down in the playbook.

2. Near square, write down the things in your life that are trying to attack you.

3. Near circle, write down how you will defend yourself against them. Make sure to use Biblical references. (i.e. Circle: I will not let negative thoughts stay in my mind. Reference: 2 Corinthians 10:5)

4. Guess what? All those things that were sent to attack you have already been defeated when Jesus went to the cross! In the "home" score box, write, "I WIN!"

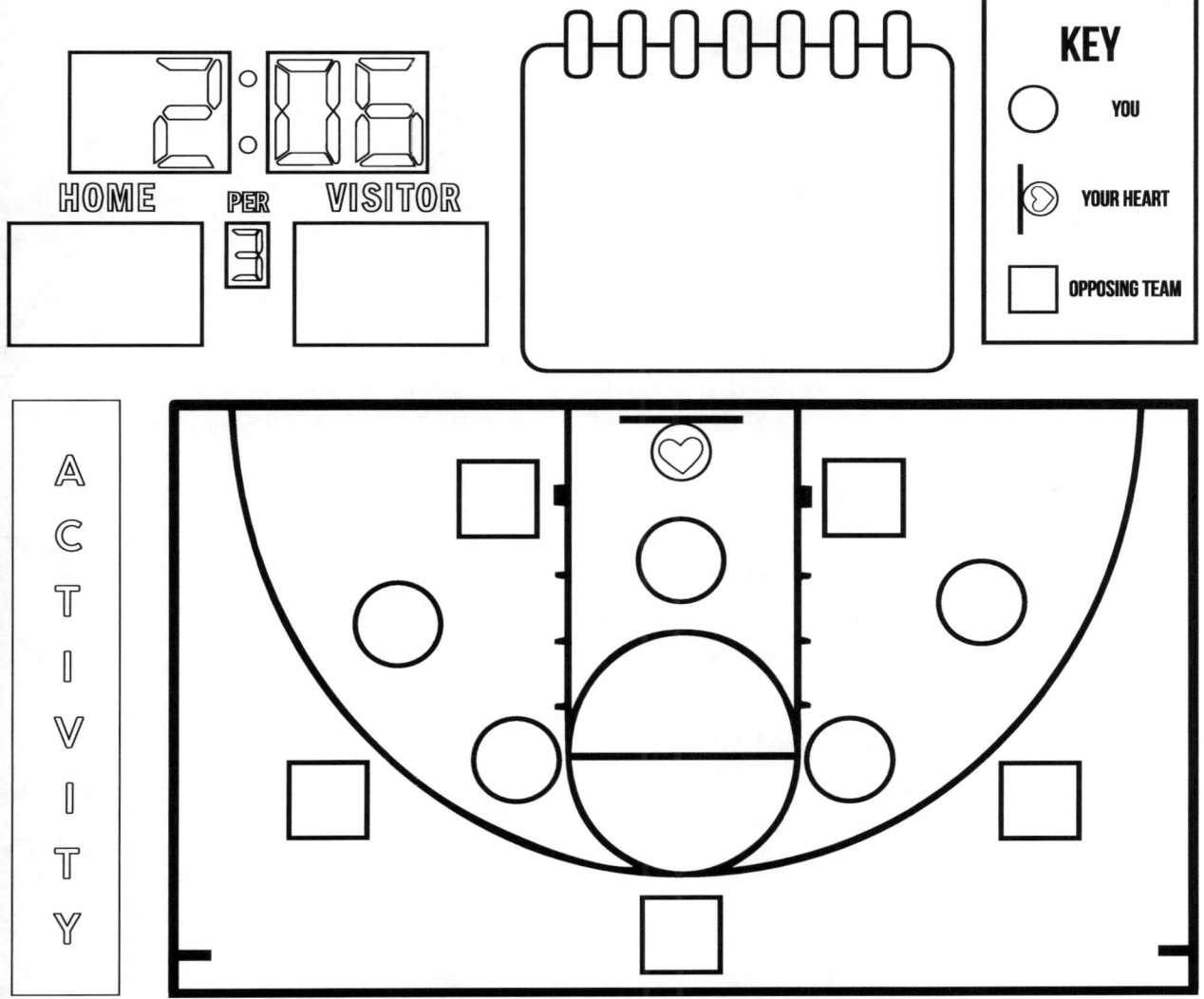

color playlist

COLOR PICK

SONGS

LECRAE // WORTH IT

SEAN JOHNSON // SAVE ME

LAUREN DAIGLE // YOU SAY

AMANDA COOK // PEACE

YOUR PICK

SONGS

COLOR PICK

PASTOR SARAH JAKES ROBERTS // LOST AND FOUND - PART 2

PASTOR MIKE TODD // PEACE UNDER PRESSURE :: FRUITFULL

PASTOR STEVEN FURTICK // 3 HABITS OF A HEALTHY HEART

PASTOR SARAH JAKES ROBERTS // YOU KNOW BETTER

HEATHER LINDSEY // HE'S JUST NOT THAT INTO YOU

YOUTUBE

YOUR PICK

YOUTUBE

encouragement

You are loved by God. You are wonderfully made. You are beautiful and you are worth so much more than settling for gray. He can't have you anymore. You're too valuable to put yourself on the clearance rack. Sis, you are the righteousness of God in Christ. You are worth far more than rubies. Can't you see it? Can't you see where God is calling you to? Drop the weight. Get rid of the burdens so you can be free. So you can fly again, breathe again, live again— this time, in color.

prayers

chapter feels

_____

_____

_____

_____

_____

_____

_____

_____

_____

_____

_____

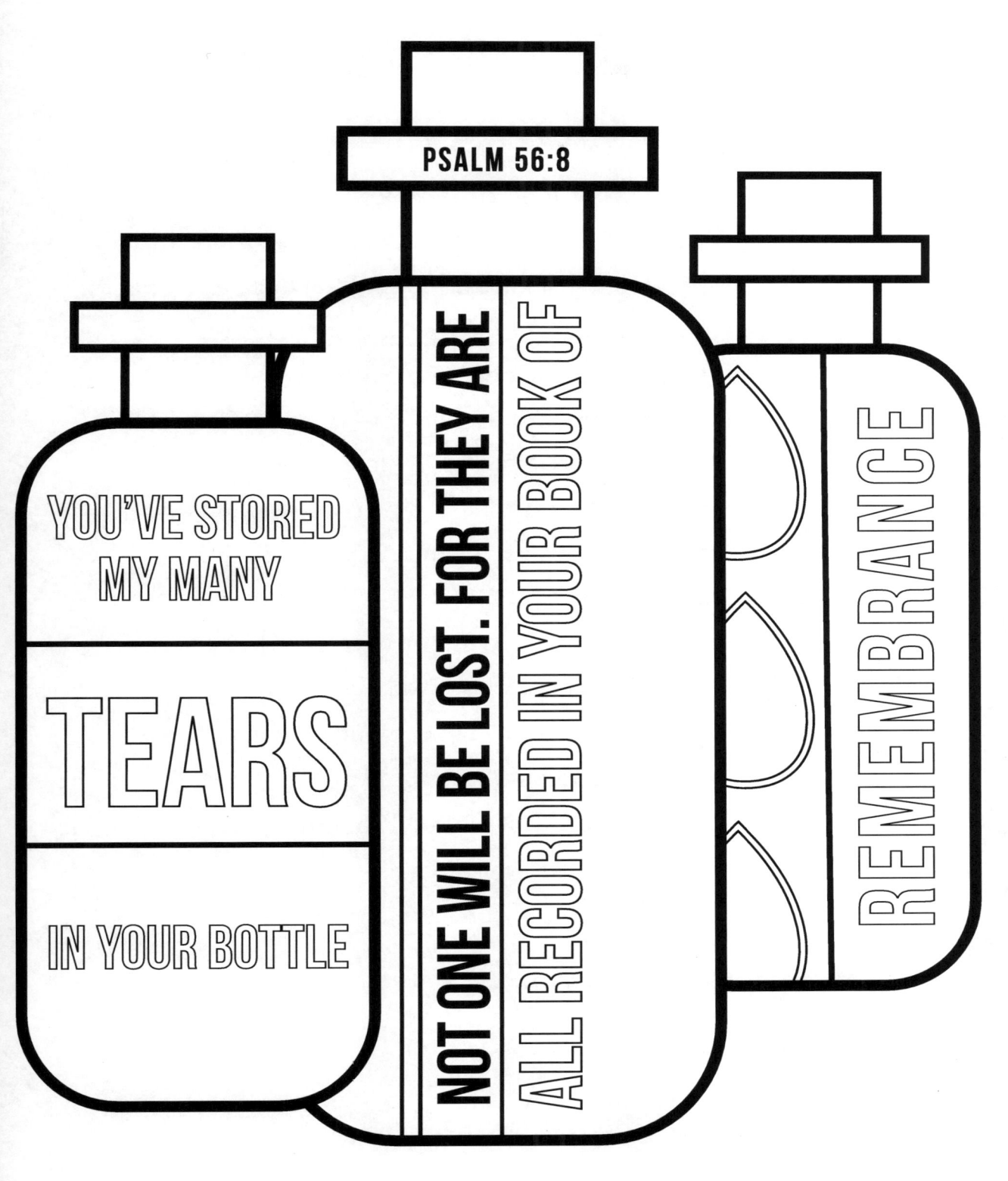

gray tears

Sis! How are you feeling? This chapter may have brought up some sad memories for you. Or maybe you're past the crying stage. Wherever you are, just know that you are loved, called and chosen by God. Whatever lies you've adopted into your identity are false and I cast them down right now, in Jesus' name. It's time for you to cast them down too! This is a war for your soul, sis. It's much bigger than a situationship, a bad friendship, or reoccurring negative thoughts. The enemy wants your mind and if you surround yourself with negativity then he will surely have it. "Fix your thoughts on what is true, and honorable, and right, and pure, and lovely, and admirable. Think about things that are excellent and worthy of praise" (Philippians 4:8) so that you can continue to live in color...

peace.

Have you ever felt condemned? It's like no matter what you do, it's never good enough— you're never good enough. Well, sis, condemnation is a trick of the devil. While we do need to take responsibility for our actions and repent, God does not condemn by telling us how bad we are. He convicts us and leads us to make better choices the next time we're faced with a similar situation. You may feel stuck in a situationship that you know is wrong and you want to get out but you also want to stay. You want to be obedient to God but you also don't want to feel lonely. In this section, we'll discuss the battle in our minds, changing the narrative of negative thinking, and heeding to Our Daddy's instruction and correction.

REFLECTION

Has the enemy ever tried to wage war on your mind? What lies did he try to tell you about yourself? Did you accept the lies or did you fight back with God's Word?

Write down five positive qualities about yourself. Then find a mirror and read them out loud to yourself 3 times. Now, find five positive things that God says about you in His word (Google it if you have to). Write them down and repeat all ten statements out loud, while looking at yourself in the mirror.

After reading the section about discipline, how do you feel? How would you describe God's discipline? What is the importance of it?

How have you responded to Our Daddy's discipline in the past? Have you shrugged it off and ignored it? Have you taken it seriously and tried to change? Were you indifferent to the process?

Once we accept Jesus into our lives, He has promised that we will always have the Holy Spirit with us. God is constantly speaking to us in different ways (through His Word, through people, sermons, nature, etc.) but sometimes we don't hear Him because we aren't listening. After reading about conviction (2 Corinthians 7:8-11), describe a time when the Holy Spirit convicted you in order to get you back on track. Did you listen to Him? How did you feel after?

El Roi // The God Who Sees You

"You've kept track of all my wandering and my weeping. You've stored my many tears in your bottle—not one will be lost. For they are all recorded in your book of remembrance." (Psalm 56:8) I have a habit of crying in the privacy of my own bedroom floor, on the counter of the bathroom or tucked under the sheets of my bed. If I'm being totally honest, I withdraw when I'm hurt. I get silent as a million thoughts bombard my mind simultaneously. In the times that I isolate myself, either one of two things can happen. I can take that time of silence and listen to what God is trying to tell me or I can become so consumed in negative thinking that my silence slowly tears me down. If I'm not guarding my heart with God's Word, then the latter usually occurs...

What have you shed gray tears over lately?
1. Write down your worries in the water portion of the bottle.
2. Write down a prayer to God about your problems above the water in the bottle.

A
C
T
I
V
I
T
Y

PRAYER

color playlist

COLOR PICK

SONGS

AMANDA COOK // PEACE

HILLSONG UNITED // EVEN WHEN IT HURTS

LAUREN DAIGLE // RESCUE

LECRAE // CRY FOR YOU

MALI MUSIC // WORTH IT

YOUR PICK

SONGS

COLOR PICK

YOUTUBE

PASTOR SARAH JAKES ROBERTS // WHEN WINTER BECOMES HOME

HEATHER LINDSEY // HOW TO HEAL FROM A BROKEN HEART

PASTOR MICHAEL TODD // RELATIONSHIP GOALS (PART 8)

JOYCE MEYER // HOW TO GET RID OF CONDEMNATION

JOSEPH SOLOMON // GUILT AND REPENTANCE

JOYCE MEYER // FEELINGS VS. GOD

YOUR PICK

YOUTUBE

encouragement

"So now there is no condemnation for those who belong to Christ Jesus. And because you belong to him, the power of the life-giving Spirit has freed you from the power of sin that leads to death" (Romans 8:1). Queen, you are already FREE! The only things holding you back are the shackles you place on your mind. Learn what Our Daddy says about you. Hide His Word in your heart and KNOW who you are in Him so you can live your life out of the shadows of darkness and in His beautiful light and color.

prayers

chapter *feels*

_____

_____

_____

_____

_____

_____

_____

_____

_____

_____

_____

gray homes

Hey Sis! How are you feeling? Did you find yourself connecting with this chapter? Have you ever been a fixer, like me? Well, now is the time that we stop investing our entire lives in a crumbling foundation. This is the moment that God wants to give you a complete home makeover, where your house doesn't just look new, but it *is* new! Isn't that amazing? Your Heavenly Father doesn't remodel the walls of your heart so that you will be ashamed of what once was. He fixes what's inside of you so that you can be a mobile testimony of His colorful, restorative power!

the remodel

"Therefore, if anyone is in Christ, the new creation has come: The old has gone, the new is here!" (2 Corinthians 5:17) The love and life-giving power of God were shown to us through the death and resurrection of Jesus. No matter what bad investments you have made in your past, God is calling you to be a new creation in Him. When a home is remodeled well, its value is increased. In other words, the price goes up. The same is true for you. God has made a great investment in you. He has called you to do things that only you can do. Still, you have to allow Him into your home (your heart) so that He can show you your true value...

REFLECTION

Sis, in order for you to truly grow, I need you to be honest with yourself when answering this question. This book is not a place where you have to hide behind fresh paint and new carpet... **Is Christ your foundation in this season of your life? Why or why not?**

Has there ever been a time in your life when you didn't take God's Word seriously? If so, when? What are some factors that played into making you believe that His Word was merely a suggestion?

If you are currently in a situationship, I need you to be even more honest with yourself than you were before. Sometimes we want to prove to others that our significant other is tight with God when they're not... **Is Jesus the foundation of your boo's life? If so, does your relationship together glorify God? If not, why are you still with him?**

What bad investments have you made in your life? Be specific. The only way that you can make wise investments in the future, is if you're honest about the mistakes of your past. Now, don't dwell on your mistakes. Don't allow the enemy to condemn you. Instead, take inventory of your bad investments so that you can learn from them and move forward, making the good investments that God signs off on.

List the ways that you have invested in yourself. Were you led by God to make these investments or were you led by own desires? What has been your most valuable investment?

What Does Your Heart Look Like?

Below, I have provided a floor plan for you. After reading the chapter and seeing the example that I listed, imagine that this floor plan is the condition of your heart.

1. Describe the condition of your heart (you can add on to the floor plan if you need more space) by writing down what you see in each of the rooms below.

2. Line the walls of the rooms with different colors that represent specific areas of your heart (remember to use your color code). If you have room, you can even draw furniture.

3. Add doors and windows by replicating the symbols located in the key.

4. Draw your door in red if it has been locked.

5. After you complete your house, take God through a tour and allow Him to help you clean every room, even the locked ones. Write out your prayer.

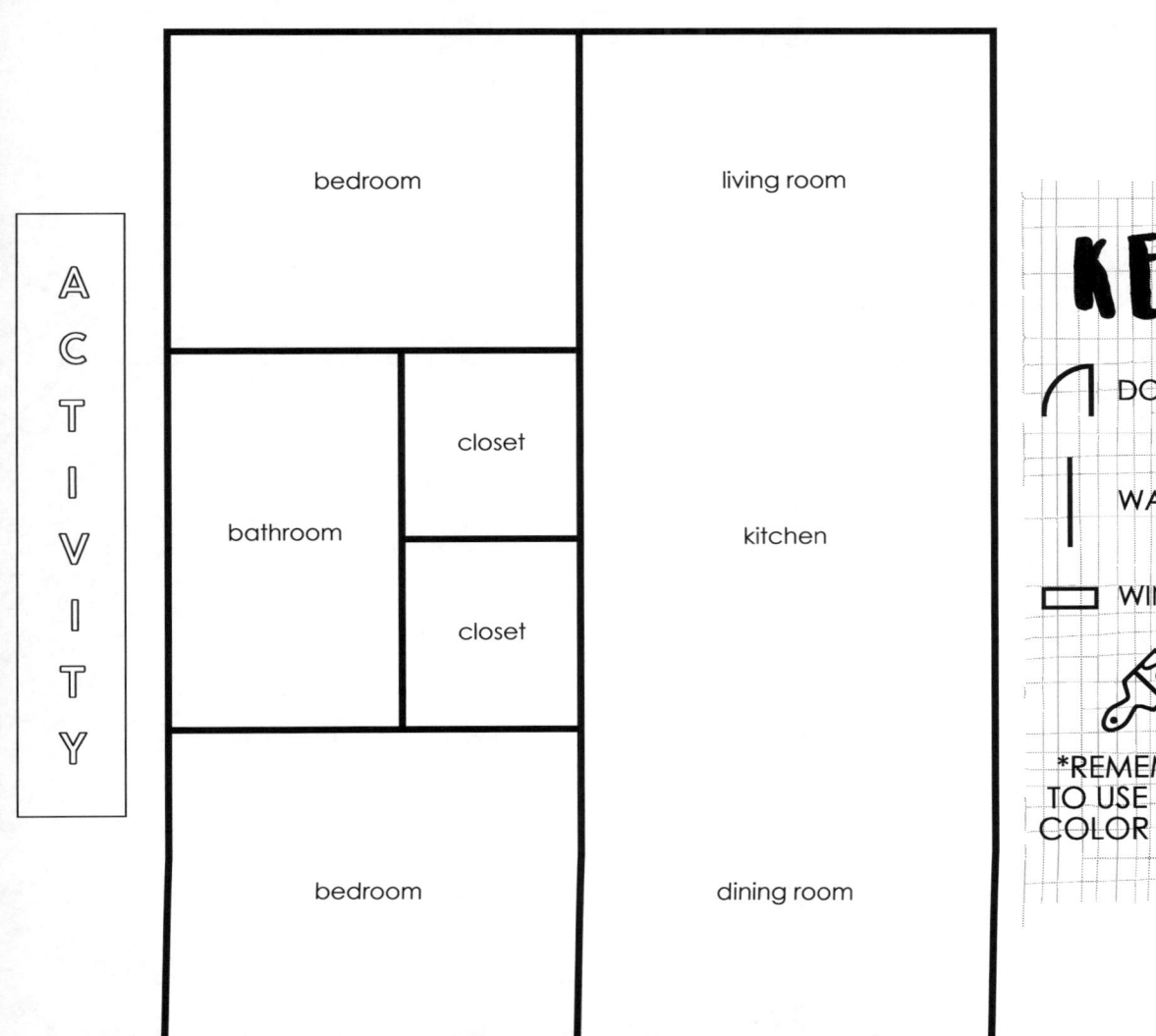

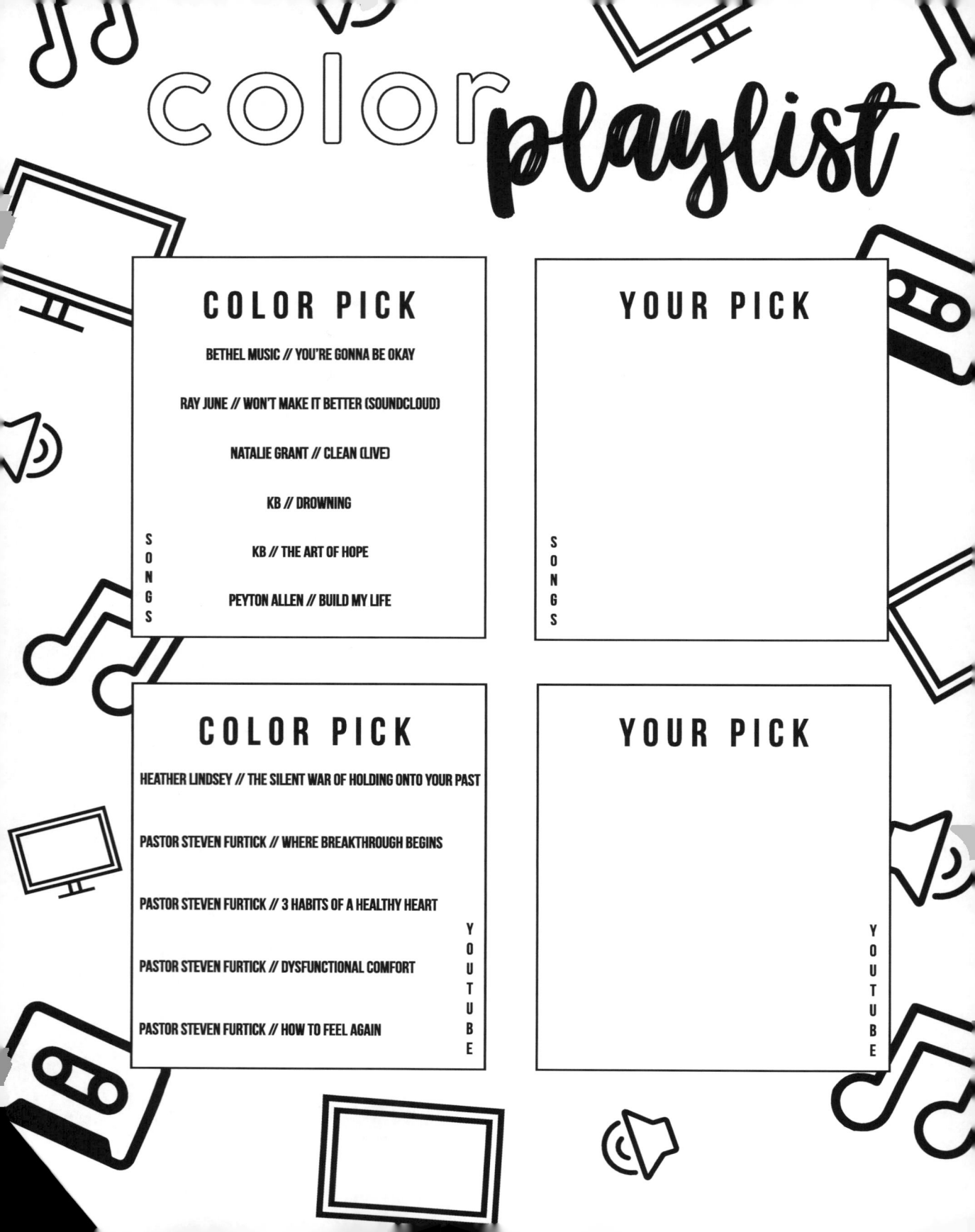

color playlist

COLOR PICK

SONGS

BETHEL MUSIC // YOU'RE GONNA BE OKAY

RAY JUNE // WON'T MAKE IT BETTER (SOUNDCLOUD)

NATALIE GRANT // CLEAN (LIVE)

KB // DROWNING

KB // THE ART OF HOPE

PEYTON ALLEN // BUILD MY LIFE

YOUR PICK

SONGS

COLOR PICK

YOUTUBE

HEATHER LINDSEY // THE SILENT WAR OF HOLDING ONTO YOUR PAST

PASTOR STEVEN FURTICK // WHERE BREAKTHROUGH BEGINS

PASTOR STEVEN FURTICK // 3 HABITS OF A HEALTHY HEART

PASTOR STEVEN FURTICK // DYSFUNCTIONAL COMFORT

PASTOR STEVEN FURTICK // HOW TO FEEL AGAIN

YOUR PICK

YOUTUBE

encouragement

Once we let God become
our Master Designer and
hand our floor plans over to Him,
He will completely change us from
the inside out. I know that change
can be intimidating but I promise that
when God is doing the fixing, it will always
be worth it in the end. Sis, Our Daddy has
invested so much in you. You are His
beautiful daughter and He desires
your heart. So let Him tear down
your gray walls so that He can
build you up in color!

prayers

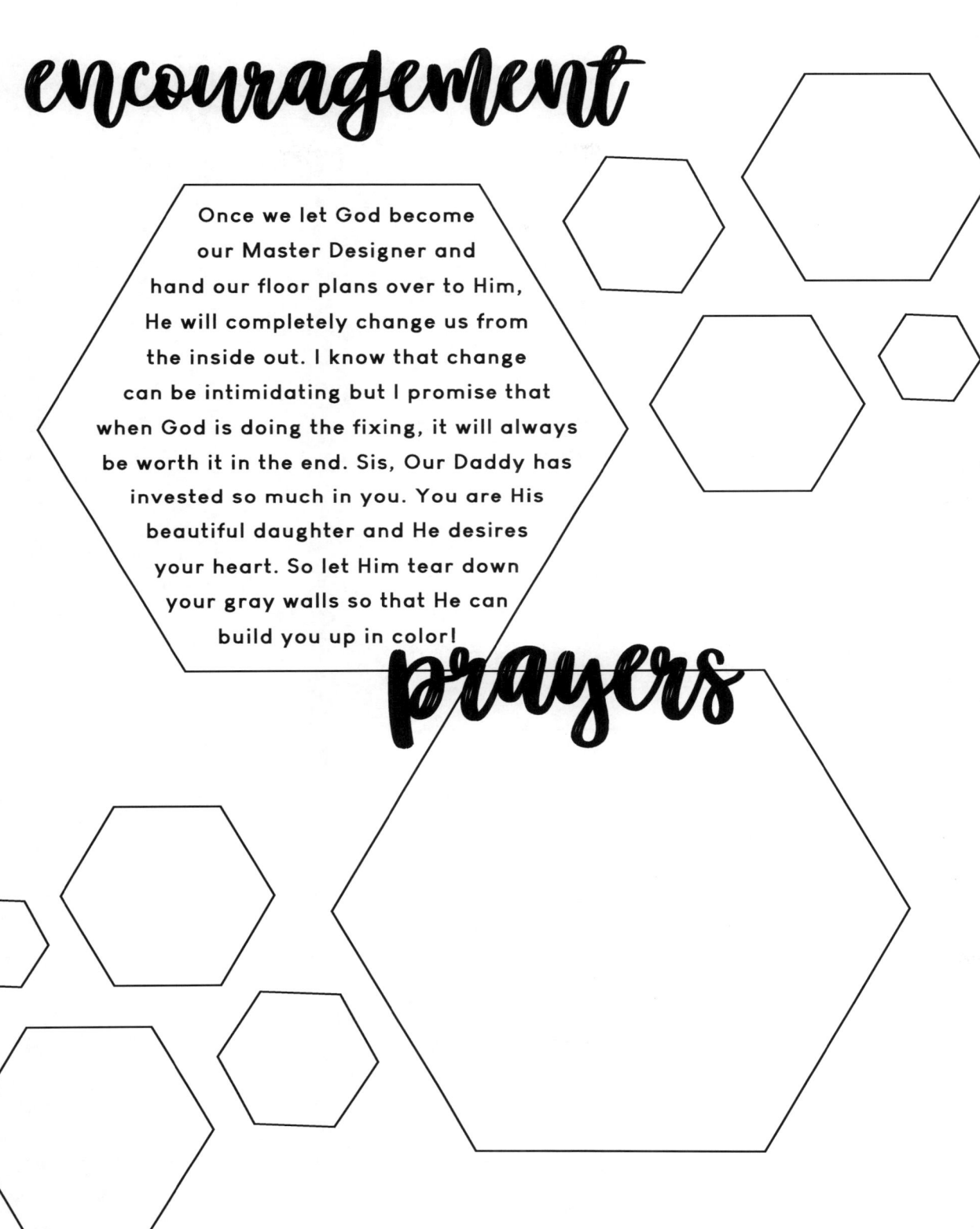

chapter *feels*

_____

_____

_____

_____

_____

_____

_____

_____

_____

_____

_____

gray revealed

Hey Queen! I know that this chapter was a little different from the rest, but how did you feel after reading it? Did you feel like you could relate? Have you ever found yourself in a place where God was pulling you out of a situation that wasn't good for you? There will be countless times in your life that Our Daddy will give you instruction. In the last chapter, we talked about the investment that He has made in you. Once you understand and believe that God values you, it will become easier to tune out the background noise of life and pay attention to Him as He instructs you on how to live your BEST life in color.

do you want to be well?

One of the men lying there had been sick for thirty-eight years. When Jesus saw him and knew he had been ill for a long time, he asked him, "Would you like to get well?" "I can't, sir," the sick man said, "for I have no one to put me into the pool when the water bubbles up. Someone else always gets there ahead of me."Jesus told him, "Stand up, pick up your mat, and walk!" Instantly, the man was healed! He rolled up his sleeping mat and began walking! (John 5:5-9)

Like the sick man at the pool, there will be times in our life when we do not truly believe that we can be healed, get out of a situation, or change our bad habits. But Jesus will always meet us where we are so that He can supply us with His Living Water. He will reveal Himself to us and give us direction but it is up to us to follow the signs that He shows us so that we can live in color. So if you want to get well, just keep coloring!

REFLECTION

Have you ever asked God to show you a sign? What did you ask Him to show you? What signs did He show you? Did you pay attention? Why or why not?

Has God ever removed you out of toxic situations? How did you feel? Did you try to stay away from the toxic environment? Did you run back to the very poison that was meant to take you out? What made you stay in or leave the situation?

Take an inventory of all of your relationships: family, friends, romantic relationships, etc. Are they healthy? How are they healthy? How do they hold you accountable? How do they strengthen your relationship with God? Do they challenge you in order to help you grow? Or are the people in your life only around to make you feel better about yourself? What lesson is God trying to show you with each person you're in a relationship with?

What things in your life serve as background noise? Be very practical. Background noise is anything that distracts you from hearing God clearly. So this could be your phone, social media, relationships, etc. **Now list three action steps that will help you turn down the noise.**

What areas of your life do you still need to say "yes" to God? Some time has gone by since I last asked you this question. **Has anything changed? If so, what is different now?**

The Matrimony

1. Inside of the wedding dress, write down your wedding vows to God.

2. Inside of the rose petals, write down any doubts you may have about making a true commitment to Our Daddy.

3. Inside of the tuxedo, write down Who God is to you.

4. Write the names of people who actively celebrate your union with God inside of the chairs on the right side of the page.

5. Write the names of people who do not celebrate your union with God inside of the chairs on the left side of the page.

6. Compare those who actively support your relationship with God to the ones who don't. Who takes up more seats?

color playlist

COLOR PICK

ALISA TURNER // SAFE

BRI BABINEAUX // MY EVERYTHING

RAY JUNE // NOT ALONE (SOUNDCLOUD)

SARAH REEVES // ALWAYS BEEN YOU

TASHA COBBS LEONARD // GRACE

SHEKINAH GLORY // SAY YES

S O N G S

YOUR PICK

S O N G S

COLOR PICK

BISHOP T.D JAKES // WILT THOU BE MADE WHOLE

PASTOR SARAH JAKES ROBERTS // MAKE YOUR BED

PASTOR SARAH JAKES ROBERTS // MIRROR MIRROR

PASTOR STEVEN FURTICK // IT HAD TO HAPPEN

PASTOR MICHAEL TODD // THE MISSING LINK

Y O U T U B E

YOUR PICK

Y O U T U B E

encouragement

Journal entries, wedding ceremonies, and signs. Whew! Sis, I just want you to be encouraged that at whatever stage you may find yourself at, you CAN be well! There are situations and people who will come into your life to do you harm. So always ask God to clearly show you the people He sends and the ones He doesn't. You can be free and you can be healed but you also have to be practical. You have to choose God, daily. So keep choosing His way so you can live your life in color!

prayers

chapter *feels*

_____

_____

_____

_____

_____

_____

_____

_____

_____

_____

_____

_____

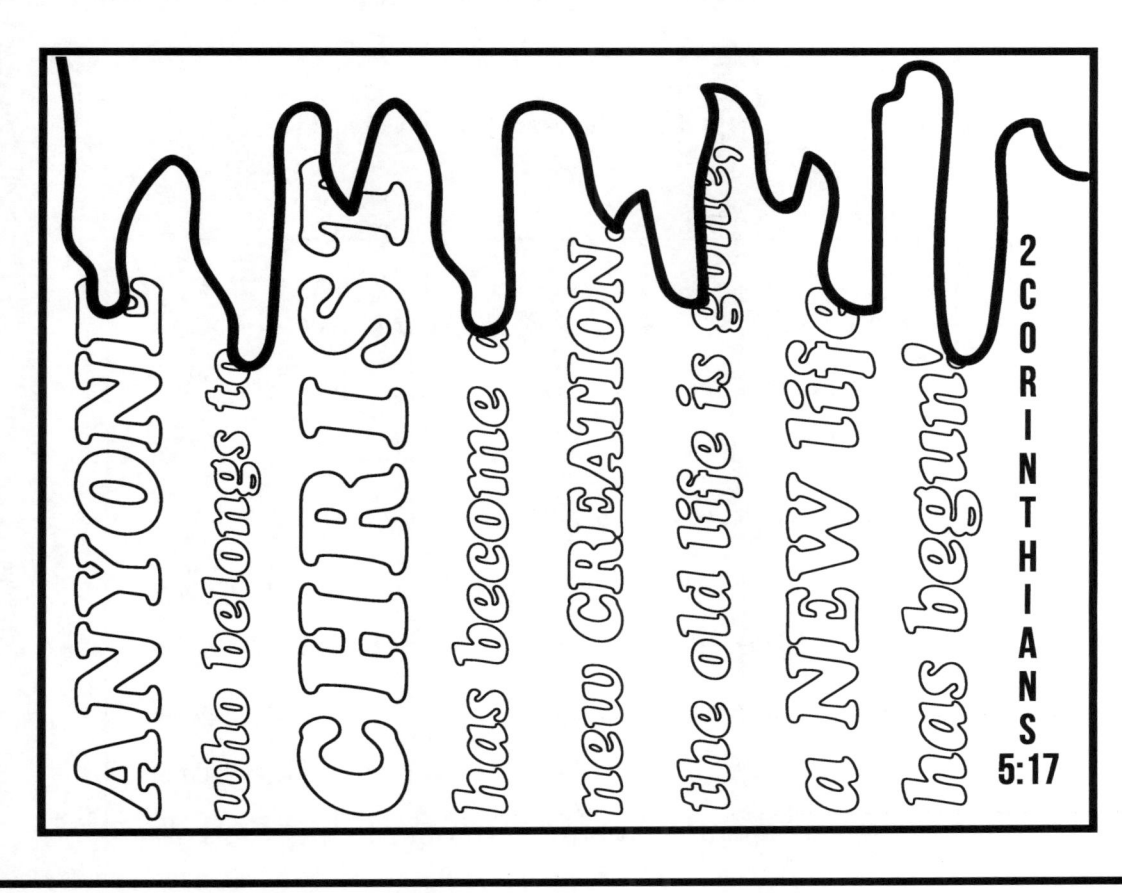

ANYONE who belongs to CHRIST has become a new CREATION the old life is gone; a NEW life has begun! 2 CORINTHIANS 5:17

living color

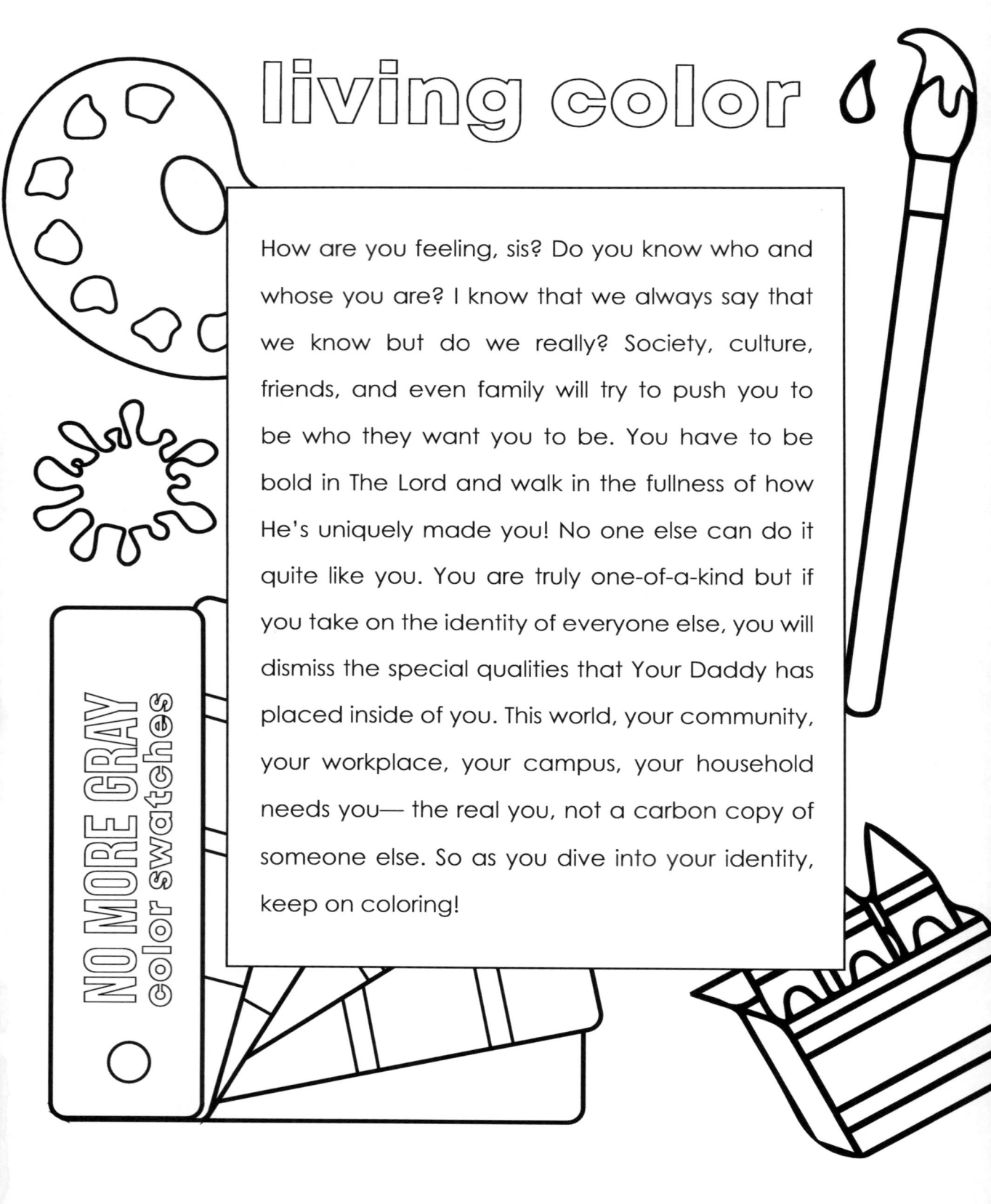

NO MORE GRAY
color swatches

How are you feeling, sis? Do you know who and whose you are? I know that we always say that we know but do we really? Society, culture, friends, and even family will try to push you to be who they want you to be. You have to be bold in The Lord and walk in the fullness of how He's uniquely made you! No one else can do it quite like you. You are truly one-of-a-kind but if you take on the identity of everyone else, you will dismiss the special qualities that Your Daddy has placed inside of you. This world, your community, your workplace, your campus, your household needs you— the real you, not a carbon copy of someone else. So as you dive into your identity, keep on coloring!

identified

Identity can seem difficult to navigate when the world is always telling you who we should or should not be. Figuring out who you are can get even more tricky when people who are close to you don't push you to be who God has called you to be. Often, we live our lives as clones, never truly knowing who we are or how much we're worth. When we don't know who we are, other people will tell us. In some cases, we'll accept what they say and attach it to how we view ourselves. Instead, we need to stand firm in what The Word of God tells us about ourselves and walk in the authority of who He has called us to be.

REFLECTION

How do you define who you are? Do you define yourself by your strengths and weaknesses or do you define yourself by God's Word? What does God's Word say about you?

Have you allowed your insecurities to suffocate who God has called you to be? If so, why? How have your insecurities helped or hindered the relationship you have with Your Father? How have those same insecurities affected your other relationships?

Have you ever allowed others to come into your life and create an identity for you because you didn't know who you were? What have people said about you that you adopted as your personality? How did their words affect the way you carried yourself?

Have there been times in your life when you found yourself chasing purpose more than you were pursuing a relationship with God? What made purpose appear more attractive to you than The One who created it?

What have your actions been showing the people you come in contact with? Do your actions match your identity as God's daughter? How so? How not?

Walking Billboard

1. In the small signs, write down what other people have said about you or what they expect from you. Think about whether you have adopted their thoughts or not.

2. Color the small signs **black** if they do not line up with God's Word.

3. In the billboard, write down what God says about you (Find out what God says by studying His Word). Have you adopted His thoughts about you yet? If so, color the billboard **green**. If you haven't, color the billboard **red**. If you have identified with some of His thoughts about you but you still feel pressured to perform instead of being who He made you to be, color the billboard **orange**.

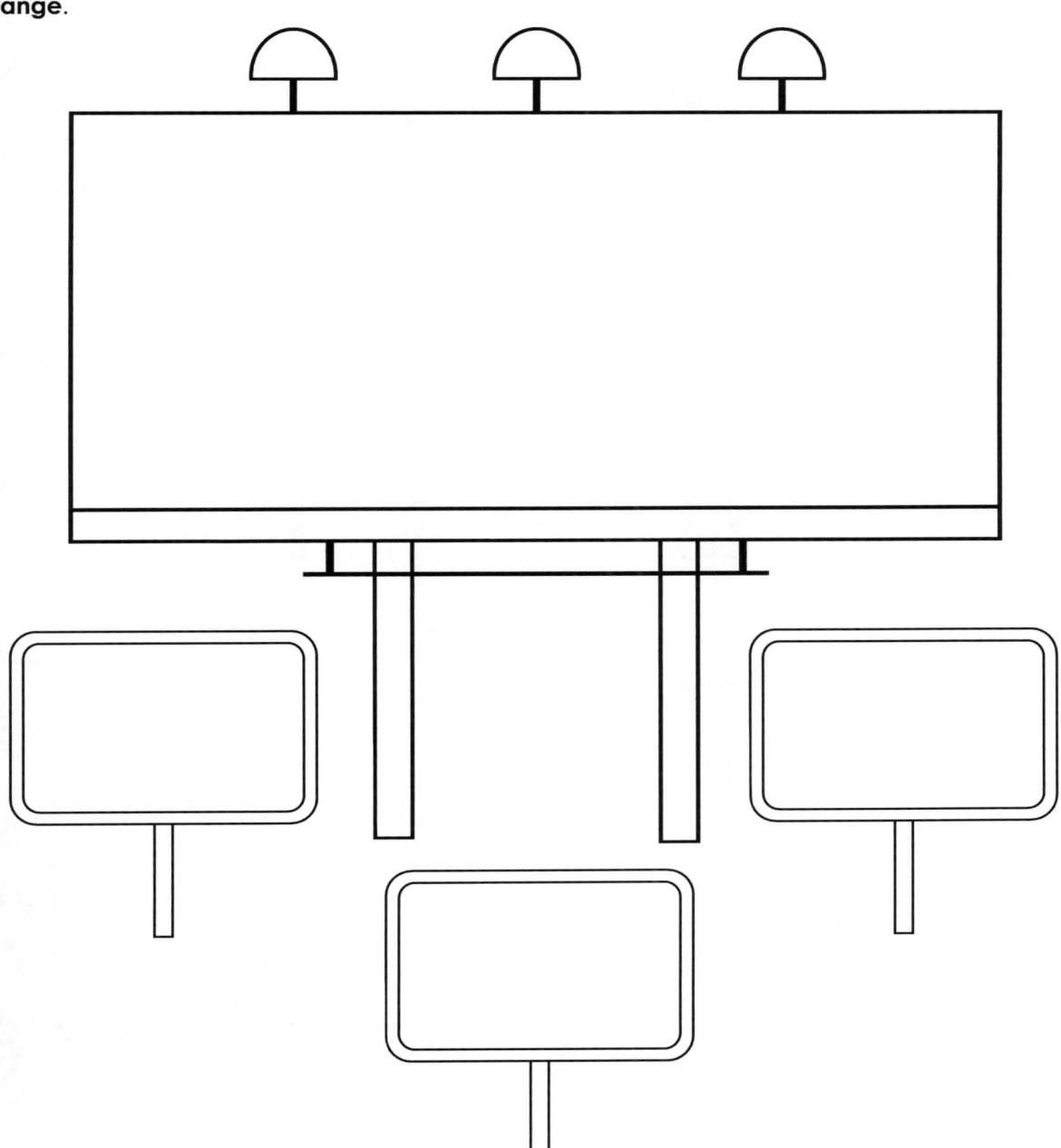

color playlist

COLOR PICK

SONGS

TRAVIS GREENE // YOU WAITED

THE WALLS GROUP // AND YOU DON'T STOP

AMANDA COOK // YOU MAKE ME BRAVE

LECRAE // TELL THE WORLD

STEFANY GRETZINGER // THE CALL

LAUREN DAIGLE // ROLLING STONES

JONATHAN MCREYNOLDS // NO GRAY

HILLSONG WORSHIP // WHO YOU SAY I AM

YOUR PICK

SONGS

COLOR PICK

YOUTUBE

BISHOP T.D. JAKES // NOTHING AS POWERFUL AS A CHANGED MIND

PASTOR MICHAEL TODD //PLANTED AN UNDERVALUED

HEATHER LINDSEY // OVERCOMING INFERIORITY

PASTOR SARAH JAKES ROBERTS // GOING PUBLIC

PASTOR MICHAEL TODD // MARKED

YOUR PICK

YOUTUBE

encouragement

Sister! You've made it so far! The more you seek God, the more He will begin to show you who you are and who He's called you to be. The Teacher wants to sit you down in His Masterclass. He wants to show you Who He is and how much He loves you. Don't be afraid to learn and don't be too lazy to learn either. Everything that you need to know about yourself can be found in Jesus. Once you make Him your Source, He will show you His technique for living a life full of color!

prayers

chapter *feels*

_____

_____

_____

_____

_____

_____

_____

_____

_____

_____

_____

painting purpose

Okay, sis! I've guided you long enough. Now it's time for you to draw your own lines and paint your own story. Don't be afraid to create or make mistakes. You've come so far! Now allow Our Daddy to take your hand and lead you as you paint. The next few pages after the color playlist, encouragement and prayer are your blank canvas. They are your new beginning. There aren't any Reflect questions or activities. This is the time where you and God can create something beautiful together. If you don't like to draw you can make a collage, use stickers, write poems, but whatever you do, do it in color!

XO,
Ri

color playlist

COLOR PICK

SONGS

MALI MUSIC // NEW WAVE

JESUS CULTURE // FREEDOM REIGNS

HILLSONG UNITED // OCEANS

LECRAE // 8:28

SARAH REEVES // JUST WANT YOU

MARVIN SAPP // MY TESTIMONY

KARI JOBE // MIRACLES

ISLA VISTA WORSHIP // 814

YOUR PICK

SONGS

COLOR PICK

YOUTUBE

PASTOR SARAH JAKES ROBERTS // BLOOD, SWEAT, AND FEARS

PASTOR MICHAEL TODD // PLANTED NOT BURIED SERIES

PASTOR STEVEN FURTICK // DON'T MISS YOUR PURPOSE

PASTOR STEVEN FURTICK // I'M GLAD IT HAPPENED

HEATHER LINDSEY // WHAT IS MY PURPOSE

YOUR PICK

YOUTUBE

encouragement

My beautiful Queen! My sweet sister! My fierce friend, I am so excited about where God is about to take you. Don't let this be just any old book. Don't let these words go in one ear and out of the other. Sis, you are fearfully and wonderfully made. God didn't make any mistakes with you. So remember my words the next time ol' boy calls you. Or the next time someone tries to slide in your DMs (or when you try to slide in someone else's DMs *inserts eye emoji*) Seriously, remember Our Daddy's words. You are too valuable, too gorgeous, too outstanding to settle for the rest of your life, living in gray. So open your hands to God and allow Him to paint your life, through you, so that you can walk in the fullness of your colorful destiny. I love you, sis! Remember to always keep painting and to make the choice:

no more gray

· ·

prayers

Made in the USA
Middletown, DE
21 June 2019